Praise for the Swimming Pigs of Exuma

"The Bahamas is famous for sun, sand—and swimming pigs."

—National Geographic

"If you make it down to The Exumas, a trip to Pig Island is a must. It had been on my bucket list for a very long time, and it was even better than I could have imagined."

—The Londoner

"As your boat approaches Big Major Cay, you're awoken from this daydream by some rather boorish inhabitants: loud, snorting pigs paddling out to greet you like a jolly bunch of golden retrievers rushing to the door when their owner finally gets home from a long day of work."

—Travel & Leisure

"The Bahamas, an alluring chain of islands surrounded by luminous turquoise waters, is an ideal place to bask in the bright Caribbean sun or snorkel with rainbows of fish. Turns out it's also the best place in the world to hit the sands with some rather unusual local beach bums: swimming pigs."

—Lonely Planet's Marvels of the Modern World

"People want this semi-wild, unpredictable pig experience and can become unbelievably and uproariously happy, despite the fact that they probably ate bacon and eggs for breakfast."

—New York Times Magazine

"The pigs are now celebrities, from fans posting on Instagram, visits from celebrities ranging from Donald Trump Jr. to Bella Hadid, and an appearance on ABC's *The Bachelor*."

—CNBC

"They don't fly, but swimming pigs are quite famous. From posting with celebs like Amy Schumer, to appearing on the bachelor and the *Angry Birds* trailer, and they are even featured in a documentary."

—NBC's Today Show

"Everyone from Amy Schumer to Jennifer Lawrence and Johnny Depp have visited the remote island in the Exumas, where the now Insta-famous pigs spend their days swimming in the clear, warm Caribbean Sea and waiting for their celebrity fans to visit. Their fame even means they've graduated from social media to music videos—appearing in Pitbull's video for 'Timber'—so basically: we give it a year until these fame-hungry pigs are on *Celebrity Big Brother*."

—Heat World

PIGS
of
PARADISE

THE TRUE STORY OF THE
WORLD-FAMOUS SWIMMING PIGS

—

T. R. TODD

FOREWORD BY DIANE PHILLIPS

Skyhorse Publishing

Skyhorse Publishing books may be purchased in bulk at special discounts for sales promotion, corporate gifts, fund-raising, or educational purposes. Special editions can also be created to specifications. For details, contact the Special Sales Department, Skyhorse Publishing, 307 West 36th Street, 11th Floor, New York, NY 10018 or info@skyhorsepublishing.com.

Skyhorse® and Skyhorse Publishing® are registered trademarks of Skyhorse Publishing, Inc.®, a Delaware corporation.

Visit our website at www.skyhorsepublishing.com.

10 9 8 7 6 5 4 3 2

Library of Congress Cataloging-in-Publication Data is available on file.

Cover design by Mona Lin
Cover photo credit: Jakob Owens

Print ISBN: 978-1-5107-6021-9
Ebook ISBN: 978-1-5107-3886-7

Printed in China

For Lydia and Sofia—
Pigs can fly

Contents

I am fond of pigs.
Dogs look up to us.
Cats look down on us.
Pigs treat us as equals.
—Winston Churchill

Credit: Howie Sonnenschein.

Foreword

The Pig Complex

When author T. R. Todd asks, "Is there more to this pig than meets the eye?" he is referring to a conversation in the famous E. B. White children's classic *Charlotte's Web*. But he could also be talking about an age-old dilemma that humans have faced since the beginning of time: how do we look any animal in the eye, think how remarkable they are, even attribute to them the same kind of emotions that we feel, and then turn around and have a piece of that very same type of animal for breakfast or dinner?

In this little gem of a book, Todd tackles the tough questions in a way that first invites us to wander with him, then reels us in willingly, almost hypnotized as we meander through the maze of sorting out our true feelings about what animals mean to us and what their rightful place in the world is.

It is more than an interesting read; it is a fascinating exploration.

But it's also flat-out funny, an entertaining read about one of the most unusual phenomena in tourism history. What makes this book so intriguing is that Todd started with a subject that on the surface seemed simple, the swimming pigs of Exuma. He takes this amusing topic—a surprising tourist attraction that has lured tens of thousands from all over the world to a remote island in the Bahamas—and treats it with such depth that he transforms it from a fun little read into a study of human and animal behavior.

Pigs of Paradise should be read on several levels. First, it is an example of how fresh ideas come from fresh eyes. A small group of pigs on an island in the Exumas did what everyone does on small islands in warm climates —they frolicked in the water. A few boaters who traveled these waters knew about it and were amused. Residents of a nearby island knew about it. But it wasn't until a foreigner with an eye for the intriguing realized that it could be much more, bigger than just about any single non-hospitality–based phenomenon in Bahamian history, bigger than swimming with sharks or applauding the marching flamingos—all just as interesting, if not more so, but never promoted with the same kind of gusto as the swimming pigs were. They had their own movie, thanks to the same gentleman. They went from being fun for a few to being featured on big and small screens, on smartphones and in smart conversations in dozens of languages.

On another level, the book explores the human connection, in treatises with experts, in Yale studies and even in a Make-A-Wish dream come true for an ailing child whose only desire was not to meet the princesses at Disneyland, but swim with the pigs.

On yet a third level, Todd asks us to make the decision. Is there more to this pig than meets the eye? Is Pigcasso an artist who can sign paintings with his snout? Is this the center of attraction for a nation that depends on tourism as its major economic engine? Avid swimmer or not, is it a beast that will inevitably become bacon for breakfast and pork chops for dinner? Or is there a deeper meaning that connects us with the animals of the world and brings us joy when frolicking with them in a warm sea?

Todd does not preach, nor does he make that decision for you. It will be yours to make, and I, for one, will be curious to see your response.

Diane Phillips

Diane Phillips is a Bahamian writer whose work has been translated into multiple languages. Among other appointments, she is a former board member of the Bahamas Humane Society, executive director of the Nassau Tourism and Development Board, executive director of the Duty Free Promotional Board, and a board member of the Historic Bahamas Foundation. Diane is also the founder of Diane Phillips & Associates in Nassau, Bahamas.

Credit: Howie Sonnenschein.

CHAPTER 1
The Land before Pigs

In the middle of paradise, with billionaires and celebrities for neighbors, there is an island populated only by pigs. For several million dollars, you can buy an island here. But the pigs live rent-free.

The Exuma chain of islands, otherwise known as an archipelago, is among the most beautiful and exclusive in the world. All in a row, running in a southeastern direction for 130 miles, these 365 idyllic islands have been home to native tribes, an escape for American loyalists after the Revolutionary War, a haven for pirates, a hideout for drug lords, and, more recently, the tropical Hamptons of the super rich.

The islands of the archipelago are in close succession; you can often toss a shell to the next cay in line. The cluster acts as a kind of dam, a giant cleaver cleanly splitting two radically different water worlds in two. On one side, to the east, the world drops off a dark cliff. Known as Exuma Sound, this colossal trench, the dark domain of giant sea creatures, plunges more than six thousand feet into the earth. Meanwhile, to the west, it's as if the sun flips a switch. The entire ocean lights up in an electric blue, so clear you can see the pink on a conch shell as your boat races above the ocean floor.

The shades of this phosphorescent swimming pool are endless: navy, baby, periwinkle and turquoise, finally ending in milky white. Words are cheap when you try to describe the water.

The Question Mark Sandbar, seen in the distance, lies between Little Farmer's Cay and David Copperfield's Musha Cay. This sandbar is one of hundreds, if not thousands, which appear for only a few hours each day along the Exuma archipelago. *Credit: T. R. Todd.*

I have seen thousands of photographs of this magical place. Nothing compares to the natural lens of your eye.

The hue often matches the depth: the darker the blue, the deeper the water. And these depths vary drastically, often in the most unusual ways. The blues are dizzying, splashed together like an impossible impressionist painting, swirling, chaotic yet harmonious at the same time. The sheer intensity of color elicits the most ridiculous metaphors, as if someone poured an ocean full of antifreeze, or perhaps bright blue Kool-Aid, among this range of islands made of limestone and coral.

The Exumas, unlike some places in the Caribbean and South Pacific, were not created by the violent explosions of volcanoes, but rather by the restless movements of wind, ocean, and earth over millions upon millions of years.

There is a reason why pirates, American loyalists, and infamous drug lords found this place. With hundreds of islands, thousands of coves, and a labyrinth of water depths, it was a great place to hide. But I think they stayed for beauty. Fast-forward a few hundred years: it makes sense that many of the world's billionaires and celebrities chose this place for their private sanctuaries, accessible only by yacht or private plane.

Look at Exuma's biggest fans, and you'll understand why you've probably never heard of it. Those who discovered Exuma didn't want her to be found.

And then along came a pig—a swimming pig, to be exact—which is where, my friends, our story begins.

The islands of Exuma, among other places in the Bahamas, were originally inhabited by the Lucayans, the first people Christopher Columbus and other explorers would have encountered in the Americas. Sadly, after the subsequent arrival of the Spanish in the late-fifteenth and early-sixteenth centuries, the Lucayans either died off from disease or were removed from the island and cast into slavery.

During this Age of Discovery, explorers would often carry livestock on their great ships to survive the long voyages. The first pigs, sheep, horses and cows set hoof on the Exuma cays around this time. In Abaco, for example, Christopher Columbus and other explorers left horses, which in 2002 were officially recognized as the descendants of the Spanish Barb, a royal breed of horses.

Some of the other types of animals—such as goats, sheep and pigs—may have been marooned from a shipwreck, whereas other animals would have been left on remote islands to fend for themselves—a much-needed meal the next time you came sailing through.

There wouldn't have been much else on the menu. Exuma is paradise on Earth, with an underwater world teeming with just about any sea creature imaginable. Above, on land, life in Exuma is limited to land crabs, giant iguanas, and nonpoisonous snakes. In fact, animal life is so sparse on land that the iguanas would become a steady source of protein for many generations to come.

The Bahamas, a country blessed with many exotic forms of marine life, has never been known for animals on dry land—that is, until the pigs came along.

Although they do swim. I suppose it all makes sense in the end.

It was during the next hundred or so years that the Exumas gained its reputation as a hideout for pirates. Just off North America, on the doorstep of the Caribbean, here was an intricate maze of islands that only the most cunning scallywags could navigate without running ashore. A pirate's life, to be sure. Those incredible shades of blue, though a source of astounding beauty today, were warning signs and traffic signals for the pirates and privateers of the day, signifying various water depths and the areas to either sail through or avoid.

Credit: T. R. Todd.

Exuma, comprising 365 islands and cays in close succession, is famous for its various shades of clear, blue water. To the right, the water of Exuma is a shallow, phosphorescent swimming pool of perfectly clear water. On the left, the "Exuma Sound" trench plunges up to 5,000 to 6,000 feet. *Credit: T. R. Todd.*

This history of piracy and, let's be honest, Exuma itself made for both an authentic and spectacular backdrop when *Pirates of the Caribbean* filmed here—twice. Johnny Depp, the star of the films, loved Exuma and its people so much, he bought an island after the filming.

The pirate most notoriously linked with the Exumas, however, is not the fictional character Jack Sparrow, played by Depp, but rather Captain William Kidd—or Captain Kidd for short. Captain Kidd's reputation could not be more appropriate: like the pigs, everything in Exuma is rather complicated and defies expectation. Was he a Scottish privateer or a ruthless pirate? There are plenty of historians who sit squarely on both sides of this fence, with evidence to back up both claims.

What did him in? The tales tell of escaped prisoners and a mutinous crew. In a fit of rage, so the story goes, Captain Kidd reportedly bashed a crewman's skull with an ironbound bucket to settle an argument. When he was on trial back in England years later on charges of piracy, it was the testimony of former crewmen who witnessed this murder that sealed his fate with the gallows on May 23, 1701.

Captain Kidd's body was gibbeted, or hung in a cage, over the River Thames as a warning to other pirates, while providing food for some of the local wildlife. Many historians disagree on how Captain Kidd was depicted and believe his trial was politically motivated in Britain.

What we know for sure is Captain Kidd, who traveled all around the world for his exploits, used Exuma and Elizabeth Harbour as his hangout.

"Kidd used to anchor his boat over on Stocking Island and come into Kidd Cove," says Captain Jerry Lewless, who runs the outfit Captain Jerry Tours.

"It's called Regatta Point now, but that was Kidd Cove, back in the day."

Elizabeth Harbour, one of the largest protected harbors in the world, is just off Great Exuma, an island measuring more than forty miles long—a perfect refuge on the fringe of the Caribbean.

Captain Jerry has a different explanation for Kidd Cove.

"He had the common sense to come to a place so beautiful," he says with a smirk.

He may have a point. Today, thousands of boats anchor in Elizabeth Harbour every year, often crowding around Stocking Island and the Chat 'N' Chill beach bar, which famously holds—you guessed it—a pig roast every Sunday.

Captain Jerry likes to say he was born on a reef and raised by a shark, and I suppose, if you like to deal in metaphors, that is mostly true.

The real story? He was born in his grandfather's bedroom, which, according to the captain, is the original marker for the Tropic of Cancer. He declares himself a "full Cancerian," born on the first of July.

I've never been able to find out exactly how old he is; his skin looks as tough as an Exuma lizard's scales from countless hours in the sun. I would imagine he has to be at least in his seventies, but he struts with the swagger of a young man, always wearing his trusty white hat with a droopy brim and colorful blobs of color on top.

He can haul an anchor from the ocean floor back onto his boat with ease and often sports a small crinkled grin on one side of his mouth (when he's in a good mood), like he knows something you don't.

His mother was known as the "shark lady," and she came by her name honestly. With an anchor on the end, she fashioned a long piece of chain into a snare of sorts, placing smaller chains with hooks along the length of it. The shark lady used stingrays for bait. When the sharks bit the rays and got ensnared, fought, and died, she would haul them ashore and use the vertebrae for jewelry. Not a single part of the animal went to waste. She'd use the meat and the skin for fertilizer for plants and fruit trees. The teeth she'd also use for jewelry—"But not the ones with cavities," the captain says with his grin.

Captain Jerry will play an important role in our story of the swimming pigs—but more on that later.

Suffice it to say, the captain is a rare breed, more caricature than character, tracing his lineage in Exuma back some six or seven generations to the American Revolution, when his ancestors first came to these shores in the late eighteenth century.

Many years before the revolution, African slaves had been brought to the Exumas as part of the British slave trade, originating mostly from Barbados and Bermuda. The "explosion" of population in Exuma occurred in the late 1700s, when thousands of British loyalists escaped America and brought their slaves to these islands.

It was at this time that the loyalists established the Exumian capital of George Town, named in honor of the British monarch George III. Exuma, but really the Bahamas at large, began to emerge as a vibrant British colony, with the island of New Providence, and the capital of Nassau, as its epicenter.

"The story of Exuma is in many respects the story of the loyalists," says Cordell Thompson, a local historian on Exuma. "They established the five major cotton plantations, and from there Exuma just grew."

It was also during this time that the first agricultural projects were taking place on the southern islands of Exuma and Long Island. Goats, sheep, and pigs boarded boats and headed to the slaughterhouses of Nassau, to feed the bulk of the region's population. Captain Jerry believes that some of those boats would have wrecked or run ashore along some of the Exuma islands, forcing some of the animals to fend for themselves.

"That's one of the first parts of how all of this stuff originated," he says.

By far the most well-known loyalist was John Rolle, the British lord and Member of Parliament, who was a powerful landowner on the main island of Great Exuma. Like Captain Kidd and the swimming pigs, Rolle's place in Exumian lore is not exactly straightforward. Undoubtedly, Rolle and the settlement of loyalists from America spelled the continuation of the brutal and unjust slave trade. But as it turned out, before his death, Rolle supported the abolition of slavery and bestowed huge swaths of land on his slaves. His impact on Exuma, and really, the Bahamas at large, can now be felt everywhere you go; odds are, within five minutes of landing in Exuma, you'll meet someone with the last name Rolle. It is the Bahamian equivalent of Smith, though in truth, it is even more common on these island communities, with some estimates attributing the name Rolle to about one third of the total population.

His impact is so profound that there are in fact two towns on Great Exuma named after John Rolle—Rolleville and Rolletown—creating untold confusion for newcomers to the island.

Once slavery ended across the British Empire in 1838, and the cotton plantations closed, Exuma became a major producer of salt for the booming codfish industry in New England, Canada, and as far away as Norway and Finland. The people, now free, carried on as farmers and worked the land, living in peace. That is, until the Second World War arrived on these shores.

"My father worked on the American base," recalls Thompson, who was born in 1944, just three years after it opened. "The soldiers there were German submarine hunters. They used special planes that would go out into the Atlantic, because there was a lot of submarine activity in this part of the world."

The base was located just outside George Town, at what is now known as the "fish dry," where you can still find old rusty ships and tankers, relics and reminders of the past.

The American base brought tremendous employment and prosperity to the island, so when the military left, many Exumians had to depart to Nassau or elsewhere to seek a job, or find another way to make a living.

But the people of Exuma have always been a hearty folk. It wasn't until around the 1940s that parts of the island got power.

Before a bridge was built, a wooden barge connected Little Exuma, where Captain Jerry is from, with the main island of Great Exuma. A long, thick rope was tied to each end of the crossing. Appropriately, the hamlet

Captain Jerry Lewless, who claims he was "born on a reef and raised by a shark," remembers a time when there was no power or running water in the islands of Exuma. Today, the swimming pigs have helped make Exuma a modern tourist destination. *Credit: T. R. Todd.*

at the water's edge in Little Exuma is known as The Ferry, harking back to a time when it could take up to an hour for the barge to reach you on one end and bring you over to the other side.

"Life was tough," says Captain Jerry. "Water was a problem when I was a boy. Finding fresh water. You didn't have the right equipment to dig wells at the time, so everything was done by paddling, sculling, and sailing. You had to find the water. And sometimes there was no rain. So farming was a hard thing. And everyone had to work. Boys. Girls. Before we went to school, we had to go get water for the kitchen to last the whole day. And then we went to school. And after school, we didn't come home. We had to go to the farm. And when we came from the farm, we didn't come home empty-handed. We had to bring bundles of wood. So things were tough. They weren't that easy."

In 1958, the first hotel opened on Exuma, known as the Peace & Plenty, which still exists today. Its opening marked the first organized effort in the tourism industry.

Exuma once again became an escape for adventurers, explorers, and those who did not want to be found, albeit for different reasons. Jackie Kennedy Onassis, Mickey Mantle, Prince Philip, and a long list of Hollywood elite gradually began to discover this paradise—before the snap, the selfie, the social media, and the swimming pigs took over.

Meanwhile, out in the smaller islands, another destination was taking shape, one that would help define the future of the area. While the Staniel Cay Yacht Club can trace its history back to the 1950s, the island truly began to take shape in the early 1960s. That was when Joe Hocher and Bob Chamberlain bought into the island and began developing cottages and a marina.

"There was nothing back then," says David Hocher, the son of Joe Hocher, who now runs the Staniel Yacht Club. "It was a hope that if you build it, they will come, maybe, and they did. Exuma is a hard place to ignore. It's a great neighborhood; a natural traversing point for boats to go from the shallow water of the banks to the deep water of the sound. So this became a stopover point for sailors."

Growing up on the island in the 1970s and '80s, Hocher recalls running around the island without a care—just make it back by sunset. He remembers the airport was built at this time; the airstrip was just being paved. It was a childhood of homeschooling, fishing, and living the island life. Days were spent searching for coco plums and sea grapes, and spearing fish on the weekends. Tourism was in its infancy then, a far cry from the hysteria of the swimming pigs. With so few people around, you came and went as you wished, grabbing a bite to eat or a drink of water from someone's house. And although Hocher would have lived a life of relative privilege, this sense of community was felt across the whole island. And in truth, it still exists to this day.

"I was born on Staniel Cay," said Vivian Rolle, one of the oldest residents on the island. She often wears a weathered purple hat with braided black-and-white hair spilling out the sides, speaking softly between red lips and yellowed teeth. "Back in those days, it was very poor. Everyone was poor. But we worked together. All the families worked together. If you don't have, I give to you. And we reached out our hand to help each other."

Staniel Cay received its first taste of fame in 1965, when the James Bond film *Thunderball* famously filmed in a limestone grotto just around the corner from the island. Today, thousands of tourists visit the "Thunderball Grotto," dipping under the stone to reveal a cavern filled with tropical fish. The Bond film *Never Say Never Again* also filmed a scene around Staniel Cay, along with *Splash*, starring Tom Hanks.

Dozens of black-and-white photos line the old wooden walls of the Staniel Cay Yacht Club, reminiscent of a museum, displaying images of the first generator on the island, or the first car. On the ceiling hang many weathered flags, left behind by the island's pioneers.

As in the centuries before, these islands still remained unknown to the wider world.

With countless caves, inlets, and sandbars, Exuma and its 365 islands would have offered many places to hide for pirates and explorers. *Credit: T. R. Todd.*

Even today, as Exuma's tourism industry is booming, you can still feel this connection with the past, to a bygone era. Change is like erosion in Exuma; you know it's happening, but sometimes it's hard to spot.

As you power through the perfectly blue water of the Exuma cays, there are countless caves, coves, and underground networks that spark the imagination. You can see beaches that haven't felt a footprint for decades; you can visualize the proud Lucayans who lived there and drew their livelihood from the sea; you can imagine Captain Kidd anchored off Kidd Cove, stashing away his bullion for future generations to discover. Head toward Rolletown, and you'll find the overgrown stone walls of homes and plantations, and the tombs of dead slaves and their masters, side by side.

As you drive into the small hamlet of George Town, the ghostly Out Island Inn comes into view. A haunt of drug lords Carlos Lehder and Pablo Escobar, this resort had a swinging nightlife in the 1970s and early '80s, back when Norman's Cay, in the northern Exumas, was a major transshipment depot for cocaine and flew the Colombian flag.

The skeleton of a crashed drug plane, not far from Norman's Cay, is a famous landmark on any given boat tour through the islands. Unlike the Out Island Inn, which sits abandoned and unknown, hollowed out, with many of the walls gone. But the roof remains. If those lost walls could talk, what a story they might tell.

Judy Hurlock, one of the top realtors on the island, remembers arriving on May 30, 1980, to an island where the telephone directory fit on one page. Back then, you couldn't make a call from the island without using an operator. Originally from England, Judy always loved the sunshine, and that was enough for her, despite the basic conditions on the island. She never left. Phone calls back home cost her $5 per minute, so she kept them short.

There was still no city water or sewerage. Judy recalls using a well, or people had a rainwater collection system and individual septic tanks.

The skeleton of a crashed drug plane, a popular sight for tourists visiting the Exumas, is also a grim reminder of when Pablo Escobar's cartel used Norman's Cay as a transshipment depot for cocaine. *Credit (top and bottom): Brendan Butler, @brendan_butler / IG.*

She remembers the Queen's Highway, the only paved road on the island, as an "appalling mess," but her face lights up when she remembers the booming Out Island Inn, the dances and cocktail parties that the seasonal residents used to host in their homes, and the tiny hole-in-the-wall bars they would frequent, lumbering up and down the beaten-up road in big old American cars falling to bits.

"When we finished the party on Sunday, all you would hear was little charter planes going back to Nassau or somewhere else," she says.

The summers were long. The island nearly emptied out completely in late April, and nobody came back until around Christmas. Similar to the clientele of the Peace & Plenty when it first opened, those who found Exuma in the 1980s were a special breed—from adventurous paupers to discreet royalty.

This tradition would continue for decades. The world's mega rich planted their flags on secluded islands. Everyday tourists stumbled upon this piece of heaven, here or there. And sometimes, these two worlds would collide in spectacular fashion.

In April 2017, a young entrepreneur named Billy McFarland and a rapper named Ja Rule (otherwise known as Jeffrey Bruce Atkins) tried to bank on the island's prestige, beauty, and history when they held the Fyre Festival, an event along the lines of Coachella in Indio, California. It would become iconic for all the wrong reasons.

McFarland and Ja Rule promised a luxurious festival "on the boundaries of the impossible," enlisting some of the top influencers in the world, such as Kendall Kenner, Emily Ratajkowski, and Bella Hadid, to promote an A-list concert and cultural event on the island made famous by Pablo Escobar. What transpired is social media history—hundreds of millennials arrived on a drizzly morning to a half-baked festival site on mainland Great Exuma, not a private island once owned by the Colombian drug kingpin. They posted viral photos of flimsy "disaster relief tents" and Styrofoam containers filled with plain, processed cheese sandwiches, with

The Fyre Festival, a high-profile event with A-list talent, was billed as the "cultural event of the decade" before it collapsed in spectacular fashion due to mismanagement. All that remains is a rusting swing set on Coco Plum Beach on Great Exuma. *Credit: Alina Semjonov, @alinasemjonov / IG.*

side salads and no dressing. The story went around the world, trending worldwide for hours and gracing the front pages of the *New York Times* and *Rolling Stone.* None of the acts showed up, knowing the entire event had descended into chaos. Festivalgoers had to be evacuated by the next day.

In the end, all that remained was a whimsical swing set built onto a shallow stretch of perfectly clear water, which would gradually rust and decay, a fitting monument to the epic festival that could have been.

There are other ruins found along stretches of the Queen's Highway. When I drive by them, I imagine homes, the people and the businesses, dreams and aspirations that began but were never finished, each one with a story untold.

The past and present coexist on this island.

The line between them is tangible.

There is still not a single traffic light on Exuma. There are no fast food chains, movie theaters, flashy billboards, water parks, or mini putts. If you don't pick up a hitchhiker, that's rude. These islands helped define the notion of "island time." It's more than a reminder to be patient with your bartender; for those who live here, and those who visit, it's a way of life, a reminder that slowing down, and remembering where you are, and where you came from, isn't such a bad thing.

There is an authenticity to life here. Time moves slowly in every way.

Despite its colorful history, Exuma never seemed quite ready for the future. It almost didn't seem meant for it. Time forgot this place, and we did, too.

It didn't want to be discovered. It would not be a ruthless pirate, pioneering loyalists, a notorious drug kingpin, private billionaires, or Hollywood royalty that would unveil Exuma to the world, but rather the most unlikely of creatures.

What an accident of history. What an amusing twist of fate that it took swimming pigs to make the world sit up and take notice. And it is remarkable that Exuma, one of the most beautiful places in the world, would soon be defined by the face of a pig.

CHAPTER 2
Two Problems Solved

Whether it is the light bulb or the swimming pigs, the world seems to turn on how people solve problems.

And decades ago, the people of Staniel Cay had a problem.

This isolated island floating in the Atlantic, 250 miles from South Florida, occasionally received supplies from the United States, and more regularly from the Bahamian capital of Nassau. While Staniel Cay might have had a post office, a church, a library, and a few retail shops, supermarkets and convenience stores were not exactly around each corner.

The fragile supply chain was dependent on many factors, particularly the weather, so food security was always on the minds of the island's 100 or so residents.

In the 1950s and '60s, most of the men were domestic fishermen. They drew their livelihoods from the sea. Island elder Vivan Rolle remembers the men being gone for long stretches of time, sometimes more than six weeks, if the weather was bad, as they sailed to Nassau to sell their catch. They would return to Staniel Cay with dry goods and grocery items, items the community would often call "relish," which would be served with the fish during meals.

"As kids, we learned to go out in the woods to find berries, and we got on the rock to find the scrub, and the solider crab, to eat and survive," she says.

"So that was our way of survival."

Given the circumstances, just about everyone on the island raised an animal or two, and there is perhaps no animal more suited for rustic island life than the sturdy pig. They are tough, breed quickly, and can eat just about

anything, making them an ideal food source of a far-flung island with limited resources.

Rolle remembers a time when just about everyone had a small pigpen in the backyard.

"We would raise pig for food, to eat on the holidays like Easter, Christmas, or New Year's. Someone would kill a pig so all the families would have fresh pork during that season," he says. "That was in the late '60s or so. But then tourists began to come to the island more, and in the summer, when it was very hot, or when it rained, the air with all the pigpens on the island would smell. Or sometimes the pig would escape from the pen."

And therein lay the problem.

Residents started to ponder other solutions. In a way, it made perfect sense to put them on an island. People don't generally like to live alongside pigs—a lesson the community had learned the hard way.

Tom Cay, located just a stone's throw from Staniel, seemed like a reasonable option at the time. They tried putting some pigs on Tom Cay to help with the smell.

"They would swim from Tom Cay right back here," chuckles Bernadette Chamberlain, who owns a small restaurant on the island. "They would get out of the pen on Tom Cay because they knew where the food was at."

It wasn't long before the community started to look further afield.

The sweet spot was Big Bay Cay, a deserted island of no more than twenty acres. It was close enough for the residents to ferry back and forth to ease, but far enough that the pigs were not tempted to make a break for it.

"My family had a pigpen," says Veronica Rolle, known locally as Ronnie. "My old Aunt Edna, she had a sow pig that she later put over there on Major's spot. It went over there and got fat, and we later had a feast. And then my Uncle Hansel, he would farm pigs and then he put them over there to get fat, so everyone started doing it. We never put them there to make no money. It was a farm."

While it kept the pigs away from the community, they soon discovered that Big Major Cay had other benefits: a freshwater pond and plentiful food. A banquet of wild cabbage and berries grew all over the island; it was the perfect place for the pigs.

Local after local gave me the names of people who had a pig or two on that island at one point in time—Sandy Gray, Oliver Munroe, this cousin and that cousin, an uncle twice removed. And the more I delved into it, the more realized that the earliest history of pigs in the area was really a story of agriculture and survival.

But the question is—when did they become the swimming pigs?

The answer you receive can be quite different depending on the source.

All images credit: Ann Hocher.

Overall, the consensus on Staniel Cay, the very first moment that people really started talking about swimming pigs, can be traced back to Emily the Pig. Sometime in the early 1990s, sailors stumbled into the bar at Staniel Cay Yacht Club with tales of a swimming pig. This is not your typical story of the sea involving mermaids or giant monsters from the deep. Residents, tourists, and yacht club staff chuckled, and some laughed nervously—thinking perhaps that these sailors had lost their minds—as they regaled the crowd with tales of a pig paddling out to their skiffs.

While at the time this might have seemed rather bizarre, there was actually a logistical explanation for this most unusual sight. Funny enough, there is another character in this story named Emily—and she is not a pig.

Emily was a cook at the yacht club who had a soft spot for animals. She knew all about the pigs that had been historically placed on Big Major Cay. But one particular pig always seemed to venture down to the beach more than the others.

Kuenson Rolle, her friend, was the "everything guy" on Staniel Cay. He looked after maintenance, the grounds and the docks, and really any-thing that needed to get done at the yacht club. And thanks to the constant cajoling of Emily, he also became a waiter for one lucky pig. Every day, Emily the cook pestered Rolle to take her leftover kitchen scraps over to this curious animal on the beach. And as time passed, the pig became so used to Rolle's visits that she started swimming out to his boat to meet him. It was not long before the pig was soon known as Emily among the staff, named after her number one fan.

Emily passed on many years later. Pigs came and went on Big Major Cay. Sometimes there were many, sometimes were few.

And as the clocks ticked closer to the new millennium, a new chapter in the history of the swimming pigs was beginning to take shape. Many of the residents of Staniel Cay were feeling anxious ahead of the year 2000. The hype surrounding the infamous Y2K bug, expected to infect and reap havoc on the world's computer system, was being felt all around the world. But for Wayde Nixon, along with 100 or so other souls on the island, this fear went well beyond a technical glitch—it cut to the very core of their survival.

"If crisis comes to the Bahamas, because we get our food from America, we would need to find some way to feed the village," Nixon remembers.

So what did Nixon do? Before the year 2000 came, he placed his own colony of pigs on Big Major Cay—four females and one lucky male.

The situation was made easier by the fact that Nixon's father had a pig farm in Nassau. He could get them to Staniel Cay for $100 apiece. Don Rolle, a long-time friend of Nixon, who also grew up on the island, decided to partner with him on the expense. And one fine morning, those five pigs made landfall on Big Major Cay. Nixon and Rolle salvaged some pallets from an abandoned dock to build a pen.

Of course, the world ticked on after midnight. Life carried on as normal for the people of Staniel Cay.

But the pigs remained. And they started to multiply.

Left more or less to their own devices, without a farmer watching over them all the time, the pigs wandered beyond their enclosure.

"The pen had been really near the water," Don Rolle recalls. "Every so often we would go out there to water and feed them, and just see how they were doing. And I guess they just got used to the engines."

Like for Emily the Pig, the roar of engines on that perfectly clean, clear blue ocean became synonymous with a dinner bell.

And they noticed, each time they came back, that the pigs only became more comfortable with the water, as they anticipated the food to come. Each time, they grew a bit bolder after dipping that first hoof in the water, until finally, the piggy paddle was second nature.

"I couldn't believe it," Don Rolle laughs.

"I never imagined it would happen because of their hoofs. And their body is not so buoyant. They are heavy. I never thought they could swim."

Did the first pigs escape off a shipwreck? Were they brought to the Exumas by pirates and explorers hundreds of years before? I suppose it's entirely possible. We all love a good legend, and these myths persisted for years. What's certain: the reason the modern pigs we know today ended up

23

on Big Major Cay, and the reason they dived in that water, is indeed one and the same—food. They are pigs, after all.

But the swimming pigs were far from an instant sensation.

Over time, more and more boaters started to notice them as they passed through the area, particularly when anchoring off Staniel Cay. We're talking hundreds, maybe a few thousand people each year.

It was a fringe attraction, reserved for those "in the know." In the 1990s, and even in the early 2000s, sophisticated smartphones and constant social media sharing hadn't quite come of age yet. The first selfie stick hadn't been invented. The pigs weren't splashed across websites, YouTube channels, or even in the marketing materials for hotels. So the swimming pigs lived on in the middle of paradise, splashing about in obscurity.

After all, Big Major Cay is just a tiny island in the wilderness of this archipelago. The people of Exuma had no idea what was in store for the swimming pigs. The Exuma chain of islands, with a population of only around seven thousand, is made up of a series of small settlements and towns. Back in the 1990s, the population would have been even less.

Rolleville, Rolletown, Steventon, Forbes Hill, Barraterre, Hoopers Bay, Moss Town, Harts, Roker's Point, Hartswell, Farmer's Hill, Bahama Sound, Mount Thompson, Ramsay, Stocking Island, Stuart Manor, The Ferry, The Forest, The Hermitage, and Williamstown: I would be remiss to not mention every single one, because there is such tremendous pride in each and every one of these communities, whether the population is a few hundred or a dozen.

Of course, I haven't mentioned the proud communities out in the cays, such as Little Farmer's Cay, Black Point, and Staniel Cay.

Many of the communities are just a sprinkling of modest houses, perhaps a basic general store, and a local bar.

There are more churches here than beaches—not literally, of course, but you catch my drift. Bahamians are God-fearing folk, and for the most part, every man, woman, and child gets dressed up to the nines on Sundays, and on Saturdays, too. The service is usually followed by a lunch of peas 'n'

It all started with a beach. Emerald Bay, the original site of the Four Seasons, was the largest tourism investment, by far, in the history of the Exumas. *Credit: GIV Bahamas.*

rice, grits, johnnycake, pork ribs, chicken, coleslaw, perhaps some grouper or snapper, and Bahamian macaroni and cheese (which resembles lasagna).

Or maybe there is a bit of stew fish or stew conch. Soul food after saving your soul.

This religious devotion can be felt in the schools. There is a very healthy respect for authority. When you enter the room, the students stand. Children aren't texting and snapping selfies. Many of them probably don't have smartphones or unlimited data plans. Something tells me they aren't rushing home from school to watch *Keeping Up with the Kardashians*. They probably don't have the bells and whistles and creature comforts that many North Americans have become accustomed to. But every single one of them wears a crisp, clean school uniform, buttoned up with pride.

There is a quiet, understated sense of pride you feel from all Exumians.

Communities are tight and tend to stick together. When they do converge, it often happens in George Town, where the supermarket, gas station, banks, and other important services are located. Funerals are grand family affairs that also bring people together. Most settlements have an annual "Homecoming" celebration, or a weekend-long party when large extended families and friends eat, drink, and socialize. In more recent years, the Run for Pompey has emerged over National Heroes Day weekend in early October to commemorate a slave who led a famous rebellion on the island back during the cotton plantation days.

And then you have the National Family Island Regatta, staged each year at the end of April, by far the biggest party of the year, with sailing competitions by day and parties across the entire island by night, ending when the sun comes up.

There is essentially no crime in the Exumas. If Mr. Rolle stole someone's purse, he won't get far. He would probably be stealing from a second cousin. It just doesn't make much sense. The same goes for the tourist, otherwise known as the "golden goose," which makes up nearly the entire economy. Exumians are very much aware that their livelihood depends on people visiting the island. So life here has its balance—a symbiosis. But despite all of that, the swimming pigs were never considered as part of the industry, at least not in a systematic way, for the better part of two decades.

There just wasn't much thought given to the pigs.

A big reason for the relative obscurity of the pigs was how the archipelago developed. Since the beginning, the lion's share of the population, and thus the largest sprinkling of hotels, had always been on Great Exuma, the biggest island in the chain. That's where you'll find George Town, Elizabeth Harbour, the international airport, and, most important, the stunning development of Emerald Bay.

Like most great tourist destinations, it all begins with the beach.

At the heart of Emerald Bay is one of the best in the world, an amazing horseshoe of soft white powder more than a mile long. At the turn of the century, the Four Seasons had its eye on Exuma, and by the time it opened its doors in 2003, about half a billion dollars had been invested in Emerald Bay, which included the resort, a casino, a mega yacht marina, a golf course, and a separate high-end resort community on the other end of the beach, known as Grand Isle.

Exuma had never seen anything close to this level of investment, not to mention by a world-class brand like the Four Seasons.

The island had come of age, or so it seemed.

Suddenly, the island was buzzing like never before. Well-to-do tourists were drawn to Exuma by the Four Seasons brand, and for a while, it appeared that the secret was out. These islands had finally been discovered.

But the swimming pigs paddled on, oblivious, largely unnoticed.

After all, Big Major Cay wasn't exactly around the corner. The distance from Emerald Bay to Pig Beach is around fifty miles; by boat, it takes you two hours or so, without stopping, before you pull up to porcine paradise.

Grand Isle Resort, a luxurious gated community of privately owned villas, is perched on a cliff overlooking Emerald Bay. *Credit: @grandislandresort.*

Now, the trip is entirely worth it, mind you. There are many amazing things to see along the way, not to mention it's easily one of the most beautiful places on Earth.

None of that seemed to matter, however. The swimming pigs were isolated, largely unknown, never marketed.

And then something bad happened—the 2008 financial crisis.

As the world's financial markets and institutions crashed, so did the tourism economy. Exuma was really just starting out—real estate was booming, the market was maturing. People who had never heard of the island before were discovering it—thanks to the Four Seasons. At a time when Exuma showed its greatest promise, it was also the most vulnerable. The financial crisis cut her off at the knees. And in May 2009, the Four Seasons closed its doors.

From the high-level investor to the everyday Exumian, no other event in the island's modern history had a greater impact. It didn't take long for the closure to become political. That the Four Seasons represented hundreds of millions in foreign investment was a cause for concern, but so were the hundreds of people now out of work. Emerald Bay had become the economic lifeblood of the entire island.

In stepped Hubert Ingraham, the prime minister of the Bahamas. Ingraham was elected PM in 2007, though he had already served two five-year terms prior to that from 1992 to 2002. Smart, imposing, and charismatic, he was in charge when business magnate Sol Kerzner purchased Paradise Island in Nassau from Merv Griffin and built Atlantis. Although Exuma was no Paradise Island, Ingraham knew full well the importance of an anchor project for the island's economy. No heir apparent to the Four Seasons property meant mass unemployment—and that meant angry voters.

Ingraham also knew how to handle larger-than-life figures.

For Ingraham, Gordon "Butch" Stewart, the chairman and founder of Sandals Resorts International, was like a big Jamaican Santa Claus, without the beard. At first, his thick accent doesn't quite match his pale complexion

Sandals' purchase of the Four Seasons was a transformational moment for Exuma, bringing unprecedented airlift, marketing and employment to the island. *Credit: Sandals Resorts International*

and meaty belly. But he merits a second glance. Nobody fills a room quite like the legendary hotelier. The godfather of the luxury all-inclusive and couples-only concepts, with more than two dozen properties to his name, Stewart had the experience and deep pockets needed to take Exuma out of the deep freeze.

But Sandals knew that reviving Exuma would take more than money.

Adam Stewart, the son of Butch Stewart and Deputy Chairman of Sandals Resorts International, remembers the meeting well.

"Everyone was in that room—the PM and his whole delegation," Stewart recalls. "And the government asked us a question. If you got this hotel for free, could you make it work? And that's the million-dollar question. The easy part is the acquisition. The hard part is the consistency of brand, and the brand promise, and truly delivering world-class service in a place that was completely off the beaten path."

Of course, nobody had any intention of giving away the hotel.

The point was this—Exuma, compared to other Caribbean destinations, was unknown back then. Not only had few people ever heard of it, but even if you had, there were very limited ways to actually get there.

The Stewarts knew full well the challenge that lay before them. They understood the Exumas better than most.

Today, sitting on Adam Stewart's desk, is a photo of a boat, floating in the bluest, clearest, purest water in the world. The boat is Adam's. And the water? Exuma.

"I often sit here and look at my boat," he says.

"And I tell everyone—everything that I do, I work to buy fuel to put in the boat. That's where I enjoy spending my time. My family has been fishing in Exuma since I can remember."

And he means that literally. In fact, before Adam was even born, his father bought a Bertrum sports fishing boat in Miami. According to Adam, one of his dad's most cherished memories was bringing it down from Florida to Jamaica, stopping at places along the way. And no place was more special to the family than Exuma.

As an infant, Adam was exposed to the area every year as the family's go-to fishing spot. Some of his first memories, in the mid-to-late eighties, were of endless days spent fishing, snorkeling, and wading in the most pristine waters in the world.

They would live on the boat. It was a place of his youth, of adventure. A place to disconnect from the world around them. It was freedom.

"In the nineties, you just weren't connected the way you were at the millennium, and certainly it was well before WhatsApp," Adam explains. "We could take a couple days off. I would see my dad take a couple days off. It was his getaway. His hideaway spot. And we just have fond memories of it."

By the age of fifteen, Adam had already met Jill, his future wife, at boarding school in Boca Raton. Whenever they could, Adam and Jill would fly into Paradise Island in Nassau, back when you could do that "for forty-nine bucks." Jill, who was from Nassau, would bring a few of her Bahamian friends. Adam had his friends from the Caribbean. And if the weather was right, they would jump on a fifteen-foot Boston Whaler and head for the northern Exumas to fish, snorkel, and swim. The boat may have increased in size since their teenage years. And instead of friends from school, Adam and Jill now have three children. But the adventure remains the same.

"Every year we go to Exuma. We spend a week, and that is the one thing, no matter what is happening in the world, we refuse to give up," he laughs. "There is a hugely deep, long, emotional connection to Exuma, long before Sandals Emerald Bay presented itself as an opportunity. We knew the area, we knew the people. Exuma is absolutely God's country. There is no prettier water in the world."

While the Stewarts clearly had a soft spot for the area, they also had no illusions. Sandals hadn't built its empire in the Caribbean through luck.

The good news was Sandals was already in the neighborhood: Fowl Cay, in the Exuma chain of islands, offered a highly exclusive island paradise for the company's top clients. And let's not forget about the Royal Bahamian property in Nassau, which already employed hundreds of Bahamian workers.

Fowl Cay was small and exclusive. The Royal Bahamian was in Nassau, one of the most recognized tourism destinations in the world. But Exuma? Where was that? It was a lot to digest. This property would ultimately include 249 rooms. And the overhead costs would be daunting—the whole development employs around 650 people. You have an

18-hole championship golf course and mega-yacht marina. As Adam explains, the Four Seasons had intended to also build 500 residences and condominiums around the hotel, but that plan never came to fruition once the financial crisis hit.

So in that famous meeting, Sandals had to carefully consider the government's question—could you make this work?

The answer was yes, but it depended on two key factors.

The first was airlift. Even if the world discovers this hidden paradise, it won't matter if people can't fly there.

"We knew if we could get the airlift to work, and get it in there, and if we could find enough people to work with us, that this would be a magical piece of real estate," Adam explains.

At its core, Adam envisioned the consumer being much like him. Most of us, he says, live in a daily grind, or "the chaos of the everyday." Exuma was less than an hour from Florida, and around three hours from major cities on the east coast. Just as Adam and his family cherished Exuma as their escape, maybe the world would, too?

So Sandals got to work. American Airlines was already offering limited service into Great Exuma from Miami. Soon, American Airlines was ramping up the size and frequency of these flights. Then suddenly, Air Canada Vacations, an affiliate of the country's flag carrier, announced they would offer direct flights from Toronto. At the time, a direct flight from Canada to an Out Island of The Bahamas was unprecedented. Delta Airlines from Atlanta would follow next, among others.

The bridge to Exuma had been built. Now, people just had to cross it.

So in January 2010, the former Four Seasons officially opened as Sandals Emerald Bay, the jewel of Butch Stewart's crown. Sandals spent around $45 million "Sandalizing" the property, which included adding new restaurants, entertainment, their signature pool, and extensive repairs to ensure it was up to code.

There was just one other problem—people didn't know they existed. That was the second key factor to making this work.

Sandals went all in—for the first year-and-a-half or so after opening, give or take, Sandals spent 30 percent of its Sandals global marketing budget on Exuma. For the largest hospitality company in the Caribbean, that says something.

"It wasn't even a Bahamian thing. It was an Exuma thing," Adam Stewart adds.

"We spent an obscene amount of money running ads. That would have worked out with basically an ad being played probably every fifteen to twenty minutes in North America, saying Exuma. So we really went to town and we used our marketing horsepower to get people to understand how close it was."

Suddenly, Emerald Bay was back on the map.

There were footprints again on the beach. Sandals blessed the island with more airlift than ever before. Exuma's stunningly blue water lit up television screens during commercials. The people went back to work. However, there was still one piece missing from those surreal shots of the water—a pig.

But help was on the way.

Down the beach, on the other side of Emerald Bay, Grand Isle Resort & Spa was undergoing a renaissance of its own.

Separate from the Four Seasons, this luxurious gated community of seventy-eight privately owned villas is perched on a cliff overlooking Emerald Bay. It could only watch from a distance, helplessly, as the 2008 financial crisis hit and the Four Seasons pulled the plug. Built in 2007, Grand Isle's fate was very much tied to that of its big brother down the beach, and the developer fell into receivership in 2009. But compared to the Four Seasons, Grand Isle was a different beast; because every villa was individually owned, those owners who remained after 2009 decided to hang on and protect their investments by forming a board of directors.

And you can understand why. Apart from the millions they paid for their villas, Grand Isle is the jewel of the Exumas, built to the highest standards and intended as the informal residences of the Four Seasons. Ranging from one-bedroom villas to four-bedroom penthouses, each sprawling home has a golf cart with its very own garage. A short *put-put* away, through the property's manicured gardens, hedges, and trails, is an infinity pool, spa, fitness center, bar, and full-service restaurant.

It is the perfect marriage of luxury, elegance, and comfort with the rugged, private, unspoiled beauty of the Exuma wilderness.

Too much had been invested here. The owners wouldn't go down without a fight.

Unfortunately, Grand Isle was ducking and weaving with one arm tied behind its back. Yes, it was a completed development; however, thirty-one of the seventy-eight villas were unsold at the time of the crash. It was a half-baked cake, and for it to reach financial stability, it needed to go back in the oven. A number of suitors had come and gone, but for years nobody seemed willing to take the plunge. The quality of Grand Isle was unquestioned. The natural beauty of Exuma was unmatched. Perhaps it was the ghost of the Four Seasons that had investors spooked. In the end, it was a Canadian who wrote the check, a financial services aficionado whose fondest childhood memories were of a beach.

It was a slightly different island from Exuma—Nova Scotia, to be exact.

"We only had two months of real summer growing up, maybe three if we were lucky," says Peter Nicholson, who lives in Ottawa and worked in the investment industry for more than thirty years. "I have been around the world twice, and nothing compares to the natural beauty of Exuma. It is the best in the world."

When Nicholson swooped in, it helped that he wasn't altogether unfamiliar with Exuma. In fact, he had already been investing there for years.

In the winter of 2004, Nicholson had stepped into a coffee shop on Carling Avenue in Ottawa to meet a gentleman named Tyrone Munroe.

35

He had been interested in the Bahamas for years, and through a friend's referral, Nicholson thought he might have found someone who could help get his business there started.

Munroe grew up in Little Farmer's Cay in the Exumas, a sixty-eight-acre island in the middle of the chain with a population of a few dozen people. Even back then, in the 1960s and '70s, many remote communities survived without electricity or running water. His family lived off the land—it was a daily struggle to provide the necessities of life. When he got older, Munroe moved to the capital city of Nassau. One day, in his late teens, he hit it off with a tourist on the dance floor at Atlantis Resort on Paradise Island.

After she left, he couldn't get the girl out of his head. One impulsive decision later, after chatting at the bar with a friend, he decided to change his life and follow her to Canada. In the dead of winter, Munroe stepped off the plane and onto the freezing tarmac, shivering in a pinstripe three-piece suit and no coat.

The man from Little Farmer's Cay wondered if he had arrived in the Arctic Circle.

He found that girl, and although the relationship didn't work out, Munroe stayed in the Great White North for more than twenty-five years. He started a career, got married, and raised a family. Canada was home.

And now, he was ready to go back to the Bahamas—for the first time.

Munroe never saw the beauty of Exuma; for a boy trying to survive in the islands, everything was an obstacle, even the famed Question Mark Sandbar, an idyllic stretch of beach that rises from the ocean for only a few hours of the day. Located between Musha Cay, the exclusive retreat of magician David Copperfield, and Little Farmer's Cay, this sandbar offers the closest sensation you'll ever have to walking on water. But for the young Munroe, growing up in the islands, this wonder of the world was simply a nuisance, because it meant his family had to sail all the way around it to reach nearby islands to farm or gather food, or reach the best fishing spots.

It cost them daylight, and that was expensive, if not dangerous.

Fast-forward a few decades: Munroe now saw the potential. Nicholson hadn't heard of Exuma before, so Munroe came armed with some photos. And Nicholson spotted her beauty right away. After a long chat and several cups of coffee, they bundled up in their coats, gloves, and toques. Munroe left with a check for $10,000.

"I told him to head home and get started," Nicholson said.

Clean-cut Nicholson from Nova Scotia, Canada, and dreadlocks-down-his-back Munroe from Little Farmer's Cay, the Bahamas, would soon change Exuma forever.

Munroe packed up his things, settled his affairs, hitched a boat to his pickup truck, and, in the blistering snow, started the long drive to Florida. He was terrified of flying and always went to extreme lengths to avoid it.

From Fort Lauderdale, he would boat all the way to Nassau.

It didn't all go to plan. As Munroe picked up a cup of Tim Hortons coffee in Ottawa, ready to hit the road, the local 5-0 tapped on his window and inquired why he was hauling a boat in the dead of winter.

I often wonder what that cop's face looked like when he got his answer.

Sirens blazing in the swirling snow, the cop searched Munroe's truck and boat high and low, until he was satisfied. Munroe set off once more, raising a few more eyebrows at the U.S. border, but continued nonetheless on this unorthodox pilgrimage to his homeland, more than twenty-five years in the making.

Then, with Munroe halfway to Florida, Nicholson got a call.

"I was at a cocktail party with some friends, telling them all about my exciting new business venture in the Bahamas. I was telling them what a great guy Tyrone is and all our plans for Exuma," Nicholson recalls. "When I told them I already wrote him a check, all my friends gave me a hard time. 'You'll never see him again,' they said. That same night I got a call

By creating a new pig colony closer to the main island of Great Exuma, the swimming pigs were far more accessible to thousands of tourists each year. *Credit: Howie Sonnenschein.*

from Tyrone from the road—he's out of money. 'I need another $10,000.' My friends had a good chuckle over that one, I remember."

Nicholson didn't budge. He told Munroe that he needed to make do with what he had, and if Exuma was as beautiful as the photos, there would be more money. And it was beautiful. And there was more money. The dynamic duo from Canada would build a beach bar on Little Farmer's Cay, complete with cable TV and high-speed Internet—a major transformation for the island Munroe had left so many years ago.

Although the focus for years had been on the cays, Grand Isle, a completed project built to the highest standards, was too tempting to pass up. A property of such grandeur in a place like Exuma would surely increase in value—a great investment. In May 2012, Nicholson closed on the deal to acquire the remaining villas at Grand Isle Resort & Spa. Finally, both Sandals and Grand Isle emerged from the Four Seasons fog.

Now Nicholson just had to sell those villas.

The fact that nobody had ever heard of Exuma was a minor inconvenience.

Sure, the Four Seasons and then Sandals provided some degree of exposure, but this destination was still a virgin, unspoiled frontier compared to nearby Nassau. So there was only one solution, really. Bring people to Exuma.

From the day he bought those thirty-one villas, Nicholson, a sociable and welcoming man, the kind of person who wears his heart on his sleeve, embarked on a grassroots campaign. Nicholson was on a mission. He invited everyone he knew to Exuma; he asked his family, friends, and associates. If you spent a few minutes with him in conversation, odds are an invitation to Exuma was coming. He genuinely loved Exuma and took pride in sharing it. Oftentimes, Nicholson would heavily discount the villas just to get people to come. He personally hosted hundreds, if not thousands, of people during those first couple of years, opening their eyes to the surreal beauty of the Exumas. But there was one spectacle that had people talking.

Although everyone loved those swimming pigs, it was a long trip to Big Major Cay from Emerald Bay. Nicholson and Munroe would typically take their guests to Ty's Sunset Bar & Grill on Little Farmer's Cay to eat lunch and see all the sights, and then leisurely head back to Grand Isle before nightfall. Nobody likes to feel rushed when they're on vacation. Boating can be hard on some people, especially those with young families. And it was almost twenty miles by boat to Pig Beach from Little Farmer's Cay, one way—and that was a problem.

Like Wayde Nixon before him, Nicholson's solution was surprisingly simple.

If the swimming pigs are far away, bring them closer.

After all, there was nothing inherently magical about the swimming pigs on Big Major Cay. Many animals are capable of swimming, with the right motivation. So how does one go about cultivating a new pig colony in the Exumas?

Nicholson enlisted an old friend—Captain Jerry.

"What happened was, we had a lot of families wanting to see the pigs," he recalls. "So Peter, if I work with you, I will try and find a cay close by and get some pigs out of Nassau, and see if we can train them and get our own pigs so we don't have to make that long trip down to Big Major's spot. So that is how it originated there."

Captain Jerry's first call was to Elvis Rolle, a local Exumian and owner of Exuma Point Restaurant, whose brother worked at a big pig farm in Nassau. It was a government farm, the captain said, designed to get farmers started in livestock. So Elvis made a call to his brother, requesting that he send six pigs—two males and four females—on the mailboat from Nassau to George Town, Exuma. Elvis and Jerry picked them up at the dock and drove them north up to Rolleville, to Exuma Point Restaurant. Captain Jerry sold Elvis on the idea because he thought the new pigs would be a draw for his restaurant. Elvis was happy to scout out a deserted cay nearby.

"He thought it was an excellent idea—he and his wife. He couldn't stop thanking me for it. So I gave him $400 for the pigs, we took them aboard my boat and out to the island," Jerry says.

The pigs scampered tentatively onto their new island home; it was a slightly different environment than the crowded pens in Nassau, and most certainly preferable to the inevitable slaughterhouse. Home for these swine would now be a beach of soft white sand, crystal clear water lapping against their hooves. The pigs of paradise had arrived, second edition.

But they didn't exactly take to the life right away, Captain Jerry remembers. After all, these six pigs were only six months old and about twenty pounds apiece. They were practically piglets. They weren't swimming pigs yet.

It was time to start training.

Learning to swim is a gradual process. When you take your toddler to the swimming pool for the first time, what's the first step? Splash the child's face. Get the youngsters used to being wet.

Captain Jerry called up friend and fellow tour operator Ray Lightbourn, the owner of Exuma Water Sports, to help Elvis out with the training and look after the colony. Each day, the dedicated piggy caretakers would zoom up to the beach and bring them food, taking them down to the water's edge to get them used to eating while wet. When they got comfortable with that, they coaxed them out a little farther, and then a little farther. Ray, Elvis, Captain Jerry, and the team took their time with the pigs. They didn't want to throw them in headfirst, so to speak. These animals would need to be swimming thoroughbreds in anticipation for the tourists to come. And then, when the pigs had become perfectly comfortable in the water, the trainers pushed out into deep water, until finally, the piggy teenagers performed their first paddle.

"It took a few weeks for us to teach them how to swim," the captain explains. "Ray deserves a lot of credit, because he was the main person for setting up the pigs for swimming and looking after them. Ray didn't do the pigs anymore down at Big Major's. He started doing the half-day tour out of Sandals, so you started to have a tremendous number of people every day going to see the swimming pigs."

Elvis also dedicated himself to looking after the pigs, so much so that he now refers to the second pig colony as his "second restaurant."

Meanwhile, Nicholson had solved his problem at Grand Isle—the swimming pigs were within reach now, just around the corner, really, which would play a huge role in the hysteria to come. Keep in mind, however, that in 2012, they weren't exactly a household name, even to those who worked in the media.

I remember the first time I came to Exuma. I had been working at the *Nassau Guardian*, the country's main newspaper, for about two years as the business editor, while also serving as a correspondent for the Associated Press. It was a grueling job putting together the paper each day, often with the help of one or, if I was lucky, two reporters. That meant I was glued to my desk, in a cold newsroom with no windows, pumping out four or five stories day in and day out. I was one of a couple dozen journalists hammering away on their keyboards and staring at screens, drinking stale instant coffee, fighting a never-ending battle with the long conga line of ants streaming from the walls. Sometimes a gob of bubblegum kept them at bay.

Far too often the power would conk out, followed by a collective shriek or exhausted sigh from those who hadn't saved their work.

You probably wouldn't know it as a tourist, but the Bahamas has one of the most dynamic news environments I've ever had the privilege of witnessing. The issues are real here, and the journalists are dedicated. People still sell (and purchase) newspapers on the street. That's all you really need to know. People read. They have strong opinions. And everyone knows one another. The Bahamian news has the intensity of a city beat but with the gravity of national issues. Elections are like rock concerts; Bahamians swarm the streets and city parks in the political colors of red (Free National Movement), yellow (Progressive Liberal Party), and green (Democratic National Alliance). Voter turnout is extremely high, rarely dipping below 90 percent and sometimes hovering close to 100 percent. That's what happens when you have a country with just 350,000 people or so. In a small island nation, even the smallest waves can rock the boat.

Yet despite the low population, there is an incredible amount of media. The *Nassau Guardian* is the country's oldest newspaper, but then you have its closest competitor, the *Tribune*. Not to mention the popular tabloid rag the *Punch* and the *Bahama Journal*. Throw in a few online publications, dozens of radio stations, and two main broadcasting stations, and you have Bahamians with a finger on the pulse.

I had been paying attention to the developments in Exuma, among other islands in the Bahamas, for some time now. So when Nicholson, a fellow Canadian, pulled Grand Isle Resort & Spa out of receivership, that was a big business story for a small island economy. He and I did a few interviews over the phone, and like everyone he spoke to those days, Nicholson encouraged me to come see it for myself.

I was newly married at the time. My wife and I were sitting at the restaurant, waiting for this source of mine to arrive. Sweeping in from the corner of my eye came Nicholson—tall, energetic, with a head full of wavy salt-and-pepper hair. He was wearing a shirt absolutely covered in messy, colorful handprints; I would later learn they were from his many children, and how important family was to him. Off we went in the darkness, zooming along Queen's Highway to the Exuma Yacht Club for a wild party hosted by Eddie Irvine, the retired Formula One driver from Northern Ireland. Turns out he owned the joint, along with his very own island.

There isn't much I remember from that night.

The next morning, a bit foggy, we boarded a boat manned by none other than Captain Jerry. It was one of those perfect Exuma days, when the surreal colors of the water were set off just right. Captain Jerry gestured emphatically to the landscape around us, preaching, fingers pointed this way and that, arms stretched wide to the open sky. His hands barely touched the steering wheel.

"Unbelievable. It's unreal," he would often say.

I recall he slowed the boat as we approached a sandbar that had emerged from the middle of the ocean. Nicholson took my smartphone and told my wife and me to sit by the edge of the boat for a picture.

"This is the best day of your life," he declared.

It made us smile. That picture is hanging in the hallway of my home.

In all my travels, I have been fortunate to experience many great days. I don't think it was the best day of my life. But I knew immediately that I had discovered something special.

I never saw the swimming pigs that first trip. Truth be told, I had never even heard of them. As a purveyor of information at the time, that said something. The pigs were an amusing sideshow back then, not a focal point. They were a niche attraction that hadn't been advertised much, if at all. It just wasn't the "it" thing to do—yet.

None of that mattered during my first boat trip; my mind was simply blown by Exuma's incredible beauty. I had never seen water like that before. So many of us have a perception of what the Bahamas should look like. And mostly, that perception is Nassau. That is not to say that Nassau is not beautiful in its own way—it just doesn't measure up to the vibrancy, expansiveness, and purity of the Exumian frontier. For better or worse, Nassau has always been the seat of power and business for the country. It is where all the jobs are—all the people. So it makes sense that all the marketing dollars get poured into Nassau and Paradise Island. For years, I had lived in that tourism machine. I had seen all sides of it: as an outsider, as an insider, as a tourist, as a reporter.

In Exuma, I felt as if I had been transported somewhere else entirely.

The next day, Nicholson and I separated as friendly acquaintances. I boarded a plane back for Nassau and returned to the daily news grind, to my worn-out chair in a cold, windowless newsroom in the Bahamas.

A few twists and turns later, which included the passage of Hurricane Sandy, a ghostwriting gig, and the birth of identical twin girls, I would find myself a year or so later in Ottawa, the capital of Canada. My family all lived in and around the city, so it was a soft place to land after more than five years of working overseas in the Bahamas and the Middle East.

Turns out, I was living just a few blocks down from the offices of Wealth Creation Preservation & Donation (WCPD Inc.)—Nicholson's financial services business in Canada.

I didn't know it at the time, but our paths would soon cross again.

The swimming pigs may have been born in the sunshine of Exuma, but they would find their voice in the frigid capital of Ottawa.

CHAPTER 3
An Oink Heard 'Round the World

Ulaanbaatar, Astana, Reykjavik: have you ever heard of these places? If you thought to yourself that they're all capital cities, then you would be correct. But what they particularly share in common is they're consistently at the top of the list as the coldest capital cities on the planet. Frozen right there in the middle of this unfortunate list are Tallinn, Helsinki, Moscow, and Ottawa.

For at least six months of the year, the sleepy Canadian capital of Ottawa, with a population of just a million people, is blanketed in a layer of snow and ice. Featuring plenty of museums, the historic Rideau Canal, and, of course, Parliament Hill, this town of mostly civil servants tends to fly under the radar when compared to the more sexy Canadian cities of Toronto, Montreal, or Vancouver.

I had been living in the city for its precious months of summer in 2013, after wrapping up my latest journalism stint in Nassau. It was October, and there was a chill in the air; my first winter in five years lay ominously on the horizon. My latest book deal had come to an end. I had two babies to support. What came next?

I had always suspected I would go into communications and public relations. Even back in journalism school, my professors had planted the seed—journalists make the best PRs, they said. It was a mixed message, though, with the profession often referred to as the "dark side." "Sure, give it a try for a year or so, just to see what makes them tick," my journalism prof told me. It'll help you get in their heads later on.

Learn the dark arts and then turn them against them.

The job certainly didn't seem so "dark" to me, as Nicholson and I met for lunch in Ottawa that October, comparing notes on the Bahamas and reminiscing about our first meeting in Exuma about a year earlier.

In fact, it seemed like the perfect fit. The Bahamas had left its mark on me. After all, I had parachuted in from the Middle East, right into the deep end—sink or swim. I didn't know a soul. But by the time I left more than two years later, it felt like home. Many Bahamians were my friends. I was known in political and business circles. I had been baptized by two major hurricanes—Irene and Sandy. I understood what was important to the people, what made them tick, what the issues were, what were the problems, what were the solutions. I felt invested in the Bahamas. And in some ways, I felt Bahamian. In addition to running the country's business section, I also received, in a sense, my PhD—in "Bahamian studies."

And so, with the winds of winter approaching, I took a position with his company that November, with a mandate to shine new light on Exuma.

Even then, I had never heard of the swimming pigs.

But that didn't last. I remember the first time Nicholson mentioned them. We were strolling between the conference room and his office, chatting about Exuma, as we often did. He mentioned that we needed to take some clients to see "the pigs."

"The pigs? What pigs?" I asked.

"The swimming pigs," he stated matter-of-factly.

I tilted my head and stared at him, perplexed. I think, until this point, he had assumed I knew all about them. But the look on my face indicated otherwise.

"Swimming pigs? What are you talking about, swimming pigs?" I asked.

"The pigs," Nicholson said, now smiling. "We have an island where the pigs live. When you drive up in your boat, they swim out to you for food."

I've seen so many different reactions to this revelation.

Some people just shake their heads in disbelief. Many appear confused, skeptical, or even irritated—it is all too bizarre. Others laugh and get playful or excited. They start asking questions. They become desperate to go and see them. Most people fall into this third category, but no matter what, I quickly learned one undeniable fact—love 'em or hate 'em, you never forget the swimming pigs.

You'll remember that conversation, when someone told you there's a deserted island in Exuma, where pigs swim out to your boat.

I asked a million questions that day. *Here is something I can use*, I thought.

And I vividly remember that first tour to see the pigs, those little specks of pink in the distance, plopping into impossibly clear and blue water, powering their way to our boats. The pigs, glistening with salt water, nearly jumped into our boat, hooves noisily scraping the hull.

I filled up my phone with photos and videos; I saw the looks on people's faces as they watched piglets scamper down the beach. Using their snouts, a few others carved out beds for themselves in the soft white sand, under the shade of a palm tree, and fell asleep—dreaming whatever pigs dream about on private islands.

And for those fifteen minutes or so, it was just pig and human in paradise: laughing, playing, eating, and taking photos, with the sun shining, without a care in the world. It was so incredibly novel. So intimate. In a world where everything feels like a repeat, where life is a never-ending sequel, prequel, remake, spin, or crossover, the swimming pigs felt defiantly original. Until this point, I had only thought about pigs as grunting in a filthy pen, perhaps as crackling bacon in a frying pan. The pigs challenged me to think about something in a totally different way. It was an escape. It defied expectation.

Like I said, you just don't forget something like that. And isn't that the whole purpose of marketing? To be memorable?

The swimming pigs were fresh in my mind when I returned to the frozen tundra of Ottawa in March 2014. Our office overlooked an area in

Ottawa known as the Market, and in the distance, you could see snow-capped Parliament Hill and the Château Laurier. People shuffled, slid, and trudged about in the blizzard below, bundled up to the nose, heads to the ground, only a sliver of skin exposed at their eyes.

The same old route. The same old office building. The same old view.

Amid the mundane, depressing, never-ending winter, who wouldn't want to swim with the pigs?

Nicholson hired me, in part, because of my intimate knowledge of the Bahamas and its political and corporate landscape. Ironically, my biggest impact would come from something I initially knew nothing about.

At his core, Nicholson had always been an entrepreneur. In college, he was the roommate who owned the house you lived in. You paid the rent—his mortgage. He started an insurance company before he left Dalhousie University, on the east coast of Canada, and built his wealth management, tax advisory, and philanthropic tax planning business from the ground up.

When he met Tyrone Munroe, and liked what he heard, he took the leap. Nicholson had always been a man of instincts.

So when I told him I wanted to shoot a film about the history of the swimming pigs, and create a marketing campaign to go with it, Nicholson didn't even blink—go with it. In hindsight, it all seems so ridiculous; it's very easy to forget that the swimming pigs were not the commodity they are today.

They were just some pigs on a beach. Very few people knew about them.

But it was the perfect combination, really: an entrepreneur who loves Exuma meets a journalist in the Bahamas who loves to tell stories.

Now I just needed a filmmaker.

My first call was to an old friend in Nassau named Jason McDowall, the founder of BahamasLocal.com, an all-purpose website and search engine for the country. Originally from Scotland, Jason had emigrated to the Bahamas many years before with his wife and two children.

"Charlie Smith," Jason said in his thick Scottish accent. "Call him. He's your man."

"Who is Charlie Smith?" I asked.

Charlie is a special Bahamian. Director, videographer, TV host, and photographer: Charlie has done it all in front of and behind the camera. He made a name for himself in the Bahamas when he created and starred in the show *Electric Air*, a groundbreaking variety show that took him around the world. Funny, creative, and distinctively Bahamian, it was through this medium that he interviewed and got to know some of the biggest musicians in the world, such as Lenny Kravitz, Puff Daddy, LL Cool J, and the Notorious B.I.G. Famed Bahamians such as Sir Sidney Poitier were his friends. Charlie rapidly became an affable, fun, easygoing patron and ambassador for Bahamian music, art, and culture. He would go on to feature some of the best in Bahamian modeling and musical talent, shooting everything from music videos to films to advertising campaigns. He worked extensively with the Bahamas Ministry of Tourism. In so many ways, Charlie was the perfect match for the project: he understood the marketing, advertising, and tourism angle, while also bringing his own creative filmmaking flare. He was the creative bridge between the Bahamas and the rest of the world.

I caught up with Charlie in Miami, where he had lived for years, having long ago expanded his business into the United States.

"Right away I wanted to do it," Charlie says. "Y'all came up with the idea. Y'all knew it would be something people would be interested in. It always takes someone else to realize what you have."

That said, the swimming pigs weren't entirely unknown to him. In fact, Charlie had filmed a segment about them for *Tourism Today*, a show about attractions, activities, and events in the Bahamas. But it was broadcast locally, mostly for internal consumption.

"It only went as far as ourselves," he explains.

Charlie compared the swimming pigs to the sights in a major city; you rarely, if ever, see them if you live there. In New York City, for example, visiting the Statue of Liberty isn't on the bucket list—it's no big deal. Similarly, the swimming pigs were acknowledged by some in the Bahamas, but they just weren't thought of in any big way; not to mention they were marooned in literally the middle of nowhere.

That was about to change.

We signed Charlie up for the project immediately and set a filming date for a few months later. Because large crowds weren't necessarily guaranteed back then, and we needed a consistent audience for filming, we timed it for when we already had a large group of tourists headed to spend the week at Grand Isle Resort. The organizer of the group had already been to Exuma before and witnessed the pigs, so it wasn't difficult to pump up the tourists with piggy fever. Meanwhile, with our help, Charlie and his crew went to work interviewing all the locals, a whole cast of characters, ranging from boat captains to local historians to proud Exumians.

The film itself wasn't terribly complicated—it just told a story.

Until this point, there were a few YouTube videos out there shot on smartphones. Ray Lightbourn and his son, Justin, had created a very popular Instagram account for the swimming pigs, in addition to their hard work maintaining the new pig colony near Grand Isle.

What the film wanted to accomplish, what had never been done before, was to create a polished, professional product, with real interviews with real locals, stunning video, and a story that captured the imagination.

As the filming wrapped up, I got to work on the script—or as Charlie would call it, my "mystery novel." One of the curious aspects of the swimming pigs, apart from the obvious, is the way in which they spark the imagination. We discovered so much lore and mythology surrounding the animals. Perhaps it had to do with the rich history of the area.

Charlie Smith, the Director of *When Pigs Swim*, had filmed the pigs prior to September 2014 for a local show in the Bahamas called *Tourism Today*. But prior to the release of the feature film, "it only went as far as ourselves." *Credit: Howie Sonnenschein.*

Pirates, explorers, drug lords, celebrities, and billionaires: Exuma almost seemed to have a supernatural, magical quality about it, like the color of the water.

How did the pigs get there?

That was the burning question everyone wanted to know the answer to.

And the answers were totally different, depending on whom you asked. Did they arrive off of a shipwreck? Were they left as food by explorers centuries ago? Who knows? Maybe they were, but those pigs were long gone now. I quickly realized that the myths were just as important as the reality; they had been woven into the very historical and cultural fabric of the islands.

Like the swimming pigs themselves, the story felt whimsical.

I think that's what made so much sense when it came time to pick a title. *When Pigs Swim*, an amusing spin on the saying "When pigs fly," treads that line between the possible and the impossible. What is real and what is fantasy.

And as the editing process progressed, and we received the first rough cuts from Charlie, what we had done started to become apparent.

I remember standing beside Peter in his office, reviewing the latest clips of the film on his computer.

He turned to me with a smile. "You realize that you will be more well known for these swimming pigs than anything else?" He laughed.

I dismissed that completely. It was just a silly film about pigs.

Neither of us had any idea of the hysteria to come.

In September 2014, after a couple months of polishing, *When Pigs Swim*, the first feature film about the swimming pigs, was finished—fifteen minutes of pure unadulterated swine. We released only the film's preview on the Internet for public viewing, just five minutes, along with a dedicated website and related social media channels.

At first, the attention we received was encouraging but not overwhelming. Local hoteliers didn't immediately jump on board. One particular hotel executive once told me "under no circumstances" would they be advertising the swimming pigs at the resort; he thought it wouldn't appeal to the discerning tastes of high-end tourists. Such a reaction is hard to imagine now, but that was the mentality back then.

Our first big win was in December 2014. *When Pigs Swim* was accepted to the Bahamas International Film Festival, courtesy of our director, Charlie Smith.

Not only was it a hit, winning the Haven Award for best documentary short, but it also got the attention of the Bahamas Ministry of Tourism.

Fact—the swimming pigs became a sensation because of their support.

With the Ministry of Tourism in tow, the swimming pigs hit the road.

After its premiere at the Bahamas International Film Festival in December 2014, *When Pigs Swim* and Director Charlie Smith would become a hit at several other festivals in the United States. *Credit: Howie Sonnenschein.*

In March 2015, Charlie showed up at a Miami film festival with Penelope the Piglet, a "distant relation" of the swimming pigs, instantly turning the red carpet pink. From Los Angeles to Charleston to Fort Lauderdale to Iowa, it was a gimmick at these film festivals that got local news to pay attention. What's more, the Ministry of Tourism started to throw their marketing machine behind the pigs, unlocking an unprecedented landslide of publicity. And why not? As it turned out, swimming pigs were marketing gold. Countless articles were firing all around the web. The image of a pig swimming in perfectly clear water showed up on billboards in Miami—swimming pigs are only forty minutes away! They started appearing in Bahamas tourism commercials, on their websites, on their social media channels, in magazines, and in official press releases.

The Bahamas sent out a media alert declaring, "The Bahamas is Home of the Swimming Pigs." It wouldn't be long before posters appeared for Bahamas tourism with a simple image—a beach, the clearest water in the world, and a pig swimming.

What else do you really need?

The swimming pigs were becoming a symbol of the country itself. The Ministry of Tourism had embraced the pigs—and that set the tone.

The pigs were integrated into the marketing and promotions of just about every product and service in Exuma.

In May 2015, the swimming pigs graced the pages of *ForbesLife*. In June, the Internet ignited with shots of English football star Wayne Rooney swooning with swine.

By August, we signed a cross-marketing agreement with Angry Birds, the mobile game franchise, to publicize the swimming pigs as part of the release of their feature film (the movie grossed almost $350 million). It would turn out to be the first of many viral collaborations—thanks to them, we reached millions of people worldwide.

Around this time, Gabrielle Union, in a bright red dress, was on the *Tonight Show* with Jimmy Fallon, gushing about her latest holiday with her husband, NBA all-star Dwyane Wade, in the Exumas. Also on the trip were NBA stars LeBron James, Chris Paul, and Carmelo Anthony.

Fallon plopped a photo on his desk of a bunch of them riding a banana boat. Union is at the front, head straight ahead and focused, with Wade, Paul, and James holding on for dear life behind her, looking somewhat unsure of what they'd agreed to.

"I love that banana," she said with a smirk, facing the camera with a deliberate chuckle.

Another photo hit Fallon's desk.

"Explain what is going on here," he asked.

"Those are the infamous swimming pigs of Exuma!" Union declared.

Charlie Smith was a popular target for interviews at film festivals after walking the red carpet with Penelope the Pig, a "distant cousin" of the famous swimming pigs. *Credit: Howie Sonnenschein.*

Charlie Smith explains the background of Exuma's Swimming Pigs during a Q&A session after a screening in Fort Lauderdale. *Credit: Howie Sonnenschein.*

"I've heard of this! Now that's LeBron . . . ," he joked, pointing to Union in her white hat and matching bikini. "Now these pictures . . . I think they are photoshopped. He doesn't actually look like that . . . he normally wears a one-piece." Fallon paused for the crowd's laughter. "No, this is you, clearly. Now the swimming pigs. The pigs come and swim with you?"

"Well, we go in and swim with the pigs. This is their natural habitat."

"The ocean?!" Fallon cut in, followed by another gaggle of laughter.

"Well, yeah! Someone brought them in, and they adapted. So they're just out there ..."

"Some kid is tuning in right now," Fallon joked, "and saying, 'What is going on, dude? Swimming pigs?!' But they do, they swim with you? I saw this on YouTube."

"Well, they were only swimming with me," Union explained. "Nobody got off the boat. After the banana boat ... but, yeah, I was out there alone with the pigs."

Every day it seemed like something new was popping up: another article, another video, another Google Alert. After a while, you grow numb to the screen's glare.

It wouldn't be until I got back on the island that I'd appreciate the craze.

I was leading a group on a boat trip from Grand Isle, like we often did back then, and of course we made a stop at the swimming pigs. Back in the day, it wasn't unusual to be the only boat on the beach. Maybe you shared the pigs with a few others. And this time, the visit began like any other: there was a small handful of us feeding the pigs, a content oink here or there among the gently lapping waves.

A moment later, an entire fleet of large sleek boats roared in front of us.

The anchor splashed, and out of the back of the boats streamed dozens of determined tourists, an invading force wading toward us waist deep, storming the beach, precious smartphones held high to avoid the choppy waves, their social media weapons armed and ready.

Soon, I could barely feed a pig. And forget about the piglets—there was a waiting list. I remember one of the guests was wearing a wedding tiara. She roused her guests to come together for a group photo; someone asked me to take a picture.

Pig Beach was overrun with people chasing pigs in paradise; an orgy of photos, posts, and hashtags followed, posted on the Internet within seconds for the world to see.

I often say that the swimming pigs were made for the twenty-first century. They might have lived for decades on these islands, or maybe even hundreds of years, back during colonial times. But it was social media that tipped the scales: our insatiable desire to share, to be seen, to be shocking. This need is epitomized by the selfie, the ultimate expression of "I was here, look at me"—with a pig.

That original encounter, embracing the unexpected—we all want a taste of it, to leverage it for our own social media followings. The swimming pigs fuel our compulsion for more likes, comments, and shares.

The pigs were a runaway social media train, and nothing was going to stop it.

The Kardashians got piggy with it. Supermodels. The Trumps. Armies of millennials came next, a new generation of "influencers" with online celebrity status, broadcasting that precious piggy selfie to legions of envious followers.

And, boy, did the followers start following.

The pig rush could be felt across Exuma.

Remember that second colony?

As it turns out, ownership of the beach was rather ambiguous. A local stepped in and demanded a king's ransom in rent to keep the pigs on the beach. Days later, the swimming pigs, now fully grown, had to be moved to a new island nearby, where they remain to this day.

New tour boat businesses were popping up every day. Resorts posted record occupancy numbers. The gift shops were suddenly filled with little stuffed pigs and swimming pig coffee cups, shot glasses, T-shirts, and sweaters.

The "Do Not Disturb" sign for villas at Grand Isle now said: "Gone Swimming with the Pigs."

Suddenly, the pigs were big business.

It wasn't long before Sal Ferraro came knocking at our door.

Sal was in marketing and advertising in New York City, and a few years back, he sold his share of an agency. If there was one thing Sal knew a lot about, it was branding. And in the swimming pigs he saw a huge opportunity not only to market the latest craze, but also to fill a perceived void in the marketplace.

Sal needed help getting to know the players in the Bahamas and getting his product out there in Exuma's shops. That was where we came in.

"You tipped us off on the potential. We actually had a different concept for our apparel brand around travel. We were going to test the concept in Exuma, which is why we reached out to you," he explains. "But after we swam with the pigs for the first time, we realized there wasn't a great option for commemorating that experience with product. When you got to Disney, you buy a Mickey Mouse shirt, for example, and there really wasn't an equivalent in Exuma. We would have wanted a really cool commemorative souvenir, and there wasn't anything available, at least not something we would wear when we got back to the U.S."

So Sal decided to go whole hog—The Swimming Pig was born, an apparel brand that encapsulated that unique experience.

For Sal, it was the celebrities and social media that fueled all the hysteria; there is a kind of glamour in going to see the pigs, as if it were reserved for the rich and famous. The reality is that many people with much less means can still have the experience. Sal said there is a certain authenticity to swimming with the pigs. The intimate access to the animals sets it apart from other attractions centered around animals—it is unique to get that up close and personal.

Whatever the reason, at the core, Sal knew one thing—the pigs sell.

Of course, Sal wasn't the only one with a hunch.

It happened gradually at first—you step into a gift shop and notice a shirt hanging on the wall with a swimming pig on it. I always got a kick out of that. But before long,. pigs were everywhere, on just about any product you can imagine, from jewelry, to mugs, to stuffed animals, to beer bottle openers, to everything in between.

It really did become Exuma's Mickey Mouse.

Years later, the swimming pigs would even get their own booze brand—Swimming Pigs Gin, to be precise, founded across the pond, in the United Kingdom.

"I wasn't aware of the swimming pigs growing up," Anthony Reckley says, a Bahamian who moved to London, England, about ten years ago. "When they got famous, and being from the Bahamas, people just kept mentioning it to me—have you ever been to the swimming pigs? I noticed it was taking hold."

Born in Nassau, the thirty-five-year-old Investment Compliance Officer had thought about founding a gin company for years. While

The Swimming Pig, a clothing and mechanise company launched by New York native Sal Ferraro, was the first attempt to create professional tourism products around the attraction. Credit: *Patrícia Santos, owner of @atomiclavender /IG (left), The Swimming Pig, @theswimmingpigstore / IG (right).*

Anthony Reckley, a Bahamian investment compliance officer in London, England, says he had thought about creating an island-flavored gin for years. As the pigs became famous, Swimming Pigs Gin was the obvious choice. *Credit: Swimming Pigs Gin, @swimmingpigsgin / IG.*

he had always liked the drink, to Reckley, there wasn't anything in the marketplace that tasted the way he really liked. In other words, a clean taste, infused with Caribbean fruits, that reminded him of the islands. Granted, he had a rather different experience with gin from the start. In the Bahamas, the locals enjoy sipping a beverage known as Sky Juice— gin, coconut water, condensed milk, and if you want to get a bit fancy, a sprinkle of nutmeg.

Reckley knew that manufacturing Sky Juice would never fly.

After all, condescended milk? It wouldn't keep on the shelf. But Swimming Pigs Gin? Now that brand might work.

"When I picked a name for the company, I had a random mix of names," he explains. "I took the names and did a survey on what people would like. As soon as they looked down the list, they didn't even look at anything else. They just saw swimming pigs. It was so far out there. Even the name—there is so much curiosity about them."

And in Exuma, they were now the island's worst-kept secret.

"You ask any tourist what they come to Exuma for," Captain Jerry says, "and they'll say they came for the pigs. Big gossip. The swimming pigs are the main industry in Exuma today. It is bigger than any source of revenue on the island. There is no doubt about it. And when our pigs came in [second colony] and we did the documentary, it made it. There was someone explaining it, how we started with the pigs."

The meteoric rise of popularity of the swimming pigs was a surprise to everyone. Nobody expected it to become so popular, so fast. The entire journey was often punctuated by several "ah ha" moments, where you sit back and marvel at the craze. Definitely one of those moments, at least for me, was when the attraction went international. Reckley's Swimming Pig Gin was a testament to that—the pigs were now global. Years earlier, the average person in Florida probably couldn't locate Exuma on a map, even though it was forty-five minutes away. Suddenly, droves of tourists arrived from China, Russia, Japan and, really, all over the world, with one common purpose.

In France and the UK, the pigs were integrated into packages and advertising on popular travel booking websites and splashed across social media campaigns. "Schwimmende Schweine" became a searchable phrase in Germany. Eye-catching billboards were erected in Berlin, Frankfurt, Munich.

"If you ask the average person over here, they would know about the swimming pigs," says Christian Neutelings, who recently traveled from Germany to Exuma specifically to see them with his wife and two young children.

"Germans might not know where it is—somewhere in the Caribbean—but they know it exists. They have seen it on television."

For his family, it all started with a show called *The Geissens—A Terribly Glamorous Family*. Christian said his wife is a fan of the show.

Think of it as a kind of *Keeping Up with the Kardashians*, German style—reality stars who are famous for being famous.

You love them. You hate them. You can't stop watching them.

Carmen Geiss first made a name for herself as a fitness trainer, when she was voted Miss Fitness in 1982, which is a big deal in Germany. After working as a saleswoman in one of his shops, she married Robert Geiss, the cofounder of sportswear company Uncle Sam, in 1994. He sold the company one year later for a small fortune. Jumping from TV shows to music singles to other entrepreneurial pursuits, the power couple hit their stride, at least in terms of national stardom, when they appeared on a German reality show with their two daughters in 2011. More than 190 episodes have aired, depicting a glamorous, luxurious, drama-filled existence, a voyeuristic window into a far more exciting life than our own. Or so it seems. And naturally, in one of those episodes, the Geissens visited the world-famous swimming pigs.

"The Geissens are extremely popular in Germany. The swimming pigs are just so unusual. It sounds a little bit obvious when you really think about it—of course they can swim. But everyone sees a pig and they think of it at the farm, or in the mud. I think people like the pig as an animal, even though it is traditionally seen as dirty. And those piglets on the beach . . . everyone loves that," Christian says.

"Our trip to see the swimming pigs and Exuma was such a wonderful holiday—probably the best one we've had in our lives."

After *The Geissens* aired, "all of a sudden most of the German show and celebrity producers wanted to present the swimming pigs to their various audiences. And so they did! Swimming with the pigs has become the most aspirational experience when it comes to a visit to the Bahamas," according to Angelika E. Ardelt from Text & Aktion, a German branding and PR agency for the Bahamas Ministry of Tourism.

"There is no article or travel feature on the Bahamas [in Germany] that does not carry a reference to the swimming pigs," she adds. "And I am talking about hundreds of different articles within one year."

For 2016, Caribbean Tourism Organization Media Awards awarded a story on the swimming pigs first place in both London and Berlin.

Exuma and the swimming pigs were on a roll, but our office was always pushing: more marketing, more exposure. It was late summer 2015 when a game-changing opportunity fell into Nicholson's lap—he caught wind of a chance to host *The Bachelor* at Grand Isle Resort.

Although the show's producers had originally settled on a different location, financial issues had forced them to seek somewhere new to shoot. Our office pounced. In what seemed like an impossible last-minute deal, we scrambled to put together a bid to host an episode of the show.

Easily one of the most popular reality shows of all time, *The Bachelor* had aired for nineteen successful seasons in the United States. Broadcast to millions of people around the world, with a series of spin-off shows and affiliates, *The Bachelor* has been replicated in more than a dozen countries—from Switzerland to Slovenia.

We would do almost anything to land season twenty.

The process involved negotiating with Grand Isle while also soliciting financial assistance from the Ministry of Tourism. We campaigned hard, worked the phones, and explained that this was exactly the kind of marketing Exuma needed. It was an incredible effort for just one episode in an entire season. And in October 2015, the hunky Ben Higgins and about half a dozen ladies arrived at Grand Isle for filming.

The crew took over the resort. It was a giant undertaking: I recall they had personnel assigned to just the pillows and decor. I was of course excited for the exposure we were sure to receive, but in the back of my mind, there was only one moment that mattered. There was never any doubt that Ben would be visiting the swimming pigs, and quite honestly, I believe the show's producers had it on their radar from the beginning.

When you're in my line of work, you hope for many things when groups and special events come to the Bahamas. You hope the experience is positive for the guest. You hope they like the hotel, the food, and the amenities. But beyond all of that—you pray for good weather, especially in the Exumas, where the natural beauty of the islands is so important. Almost like a magic trick, the sun sets off those surreal blues of Exuma, like God, Poseidon, or some other omnipotent being is shining down on you. Without a clear, sunny day, the water can look pedestrian. So Nicholson and I, along with the rest of the team, prayed for good weather.

Unfortunately, the gods were angry that week. We got a hurricane instead. Not literally, but close enough. It was overcast, rainy, with high winds ripping through the ladies' freshly done hair. For our team, it was devastating. We had put so much time and effort into the project, including our reputation. It's funny: I heard from many people, including Nicholson, that Exuma doesn't want to be discovered. Something about the magic of this place eludes the world. It's so obvious to those who have found her, but something, like a divine presence, will always get in the way.

We agonized for months before it aired, on February 2016, about what it would all look like. As it turned out, we underestimated the power of television.

Sure, it was a bit overcast when Ben and the bachelorettes visited the swimming pigs. But it didn't matter—nobody was paying attention to the color of the water anyway. As the boat pulled up to the pigs, Ben offered some pointers on how to feed them, how to control them if you feel they are getting a little too close. All those tips went out the window when they hit Pig Beach—it was total chaos.

Brandishing chicken hot dogs, the bachelorettes splashed, screamed, and flailed around the pigs. You'd think the women were the food. For me, someone who had fed the swimming pigs dozens of times, the rowdy spectacle felt slightly overstated. But in truth, it was perfect. Just like we hoped, that five or so minutes of television magic changed the history of

Exuma forever. Any kind of mystical power keeping these islands from the world was immediately broken when Ben, those women, and a couple dozen swimming pigs were transported into the living rooms of millions of people worldwide. Nobody was going to care that the weather was less than ideal. The conditions even played an important role in the show, when Ben famously broke up with one of his fawning singles at the Dragon's Breath Blowholes, powering off in his boat with one lucky lady and leaving the other marooned. The camera drone faded into the sky, revealing violent waves and angry skies as the villainous bachelorette, whom nobody liked anyway, was left heartbroken and alone in the most dramatic way possible.

Pathetic fallacy—the use of weather to evoke a particular mood.

It worked like a charm when Ben was faced with yet another agonizing decision in love and he strolled out to the Emerald Bay marina, the winds howling, the waves splashing straight up into the air, well above his head, to strike a thoughtful pose.

Sure, those scenes made for some good TV, but nothing came close to the pigs.

It was all people talked about.

That image of a swimming pig holding the iconic *Bachelor* red rose in his mouth was pure marketing dynamite.

If the swimming pigs were popular before, now they were flat-out stars.

In March 2016, just a month after the show aired, comedy legends Jerry Seinfeld and Amy Schumer weren't shy when they made landfall on Pig Beach—the whole scene, a classic Instagram post, was positively triumphant.

With white yachts and that perfect turquoise water for background, Schumer, in a black bathing suit and white hat, leaned in toward a speckled pig, smiling confidently, flexing her biceps like a champ; it was so different from the timid and squealing bachelorettes we saw on TV, and so typically Schumer. Her boyfriend on the right wasn't even looking at the camera—he appeared mildly amused by his girlfriend's pose. The woman on the far right of the photo looked totally the opposite—completely jovial, arms outstretched, about ready to tackle some swine.

Seinfeld was right behind Schumer in the photo in a white shirt and green shorts, also leaning in slightly, but without the bravado, the old face of comedy backing up the new. And to his right, in the middle of the shot, was his wife, Jessica, one arm high in the air, a single index finger pointed straight up to the sky.

The caption: "Group date."

Jessica Seinfeld also posted a selfie with Schumer.

The caption: "Reenacting the swimming pigs scene in *The Bachelor*."

Later that month, the *New York Times Magazine* ran an entire spread about the swimming pigs, shot by noted animal photographer Robin Schwartz.

Charlie Smith and I then arranged for a feature to be broadcast on NBC's *Today Show* that took an "inside look at this Bahamas phenomenon."

"This should be the eighth wonder of the world," one tourist claimed on the show.

"Shhhh . . . don't tell anyone," another whispered.

Sorry, too late.

Every day, hundreds of new people were being exposed to the attraction. The publicity did that, but so did the sheer rise in people visiting. That second pig colony, located so much closer to Grand Isle and Sandals Emerald Bay, played a huge role in bringing the pigs to the masses.

After all, it was the number one tour.

Droves of excited tourists zoomed across the Exuma blue, and within minutes, they were face-to-face with the swimming pigs. Sandals not only embraced the tour, but they also supplied most of the food for the animals from their kitchens.

"We always grew up reading nursery rhyme books where pigs fly," Adam Stewart says, Deputy Chairman of Sandals Resorts International.

"We know it is fiction. And the opposite of a pig that can fly is a pig that can swim. But this wasn't fiction. It had never been seen in the world before. It was the most unusual thing in the most beautiful place in the world—the two of them coming together. It just drove people's curiosity to see if it was real."

And when it did turn out to be real, the social media went "haywire."

A few million impressions here, a few million there—the pigs were everywhere, even the daily news cycle.

In October 2016, Hurricane Matthew passed through the Bahamas. I had been in Nassau for both Hurricane Irene and Hurricane Sandy years before, with the newspaper, so I knew these storms were no laughing matter.

But I also knew that hurricanes made for easy ratings.

In the lead-up to the storm, a news crew from a major U.S. network set up shop at Grand Isle. They had never come to the relatively sleepy island of Exuma before for storm coverage. Why here? Why now? The reporter, standing in remarkably calm weather, declared they had experienced "quite a few rain bands."

Not quite the portrait of an embattled reporter getting whipped around by slicing rain and high winds.

He quickly segued, saying that in anticipation of the storm, most businesses on the island were shut down, including a few tours "that draw people from all around the world."

I remember getting a call from my retired parents, who had been watching the news.

"Are the swimming pigs okay?" my mother asked.

A few clicks on the computer later, I saw the news story, broadcast to televisions across North America, all about the well-being of the pigs during this trying time.

Piglets would be placed in a protective shed; adults would have to fend for themselves.

The drama was unbearable.

Fortunately, the swimming pigs weathered the storm just fine. Exuma always seems to avoid the brunt of hurricanes, and Matthew would be no different. Life soon returned to normal. And, hey, the publicity was awfully nice.

But something crystallized for me at that moment—maybe because of my old journalism days. The endless barrage of articles and social media posts was numbing, almost superficial. This news story made me realize not only how famous the swimming pigs had become, but also just how much people seemed to care about them. That was clear by reading the endless comments from readers and viewers around the world.

People were worried about them.

But why? Globally, pigs are slaughtered by the millions each and every day—bacon, pork chops, ham, sausages. We eat the ears, feet, snouts, and use them in countless dishes and animal by-products.

Pigs are used for insulation, rubber, antifreeze, certain plastics, floor waxes, crayons, chalk, adhesives, and fertilizer. Lard is fat from pig abdomens and is used in shaving creams, soaps, makeup, and baked goods.

Many of us don't give the welfare of pigs a great deal of thought in our day-to-day lives. We close our eyes and bite into that BLT. We relish those ribs.

So I wonder—why so much concern for a couple dozen pigs, living on an island in the Caribbean Sea? What does it say about them? And about us?

As it turned out, a simple hurricane was nothing compared to the proverbial storm to come, which would more eloquently reveal this rather schizophrenic relationship we have with animals—but more on that later.

Suffice it to say, the swimming pigs were a sleeping giant; after more than twenty years of relative anonymity, these animals shot to superstardom in less than two years. When Charlie and I made that film, we had no idea what was about to be unleashed.

There was no going back to sleep for these animals.

It was clear the swimming pigs—and Exuma—would never be the same.

Kerry Sanders from NBC's *Today Show* featured the Swimming Pigs "phenomenon" in June 2016. The attraction lent itself extremely well to television, capturing the imagination of millions around the world. *Credit: Charlie Smith.*

Around two hundred miles north, right about the time Nicholson was buying those villas at Grand Isle Resort, Craig Russell was zipping along on his little boat just off the Bahamian island of Abaco. In the distance, he noticed four pigs wandering around on a barren island known as No Name Cay.

And they didn't look well. Rumor had it that other locals from nearby Green Turtle Cay had put them on the island, presumably for farming, but by the look of their exposed rib cages, the pigs had been left to fend for themselves.

As an animal lover, Russell, sixty-three years young with a trimmed gray beard, took it upon himself to start feeding them: twice a week he would collect food and water from the local restaurants. Sometimes he would buy actual "swine feed" from the nearby city of Marsh Harbour. It never even crossed his mind to have them swim, or that they would be a tourist attraction.

As Russell describes it, the swimming just "sorta happened" as the pigs got used to him coming around on his boat. Over time, tourists showed up to watch them swim, but according to Russell, the summer of 2016, around the time that Exuma's pigs reached the world stage, saw Abaco explode—a chain reaction.

"It just went crazy within the last year. I mean, it's huge really. It has really helped the whole economy," he says.

"We have beautiful beaches and water, but a lot of people want something different. And the swimming pigs are different. People are just amazed."

No Name Cay grew into a tourism hot spot. Signage was put up around the pigs, advertising "Piggyville." Every website, every pamphlet, every social media post placed the pig front and center, much like in Exuma.

Boat captains funneled tourists to No Name Cay.

A local boat rental company invested in a two-thousand-gallon tank to dispense fresh water to the pigs, complete with a nozzle system so that water was never wasted (which the pigs quickly learned to operate).

"I'm the only one who doesn't make any money off the pigs," Russell says with a laugh.

But that's fine by him. That doesn't stop Russell from finishing what he started, so much so that he earned the name Pig Whisperer among the locals.

"At first I didn't . . . .I pushed it off," Russell stutters. "But now I have accepted it. I just do it out of my heart. I do it for the pigs first, the tourists second, and because I get joy out of it. I do it because I love it."

Yes, pig love was everywhere. Abaco wasn't the only island crashing the party. Through our website and online platforms, I'd receive inquiries from tourists all over the Bahamas.

They wanted to swim with the pigs, too.

How far is the drive to Exuma?

The Bahamas is an archipelago, I'd tell them. It's a series of seven hundred or so islands. You can't drive to these islands.

Can't we just take a boat to Exuma? How often are the flights?

Well, the distances between these islands are vast, I'd explain; there are no interisland flights in the Bahamas. Everything goes through Nassau. I'd learned that the Bahamas might be a popular tourist destination, but the geography was hazy.

Turns out, requests to see the swimming pigs were happening all over the Bahamas—even in some of the most unlikely places.

Spanish Wells, located off the northern tip of Eleuthera, never gave much thought to tourism. This tiny, sliver-like island, about 50 miles northeast of Nassau, was settled in the mid-seventeenth century by the British, named after the Spanish explorers that visited this area to resupply on their way back to Europe. In fact, they built wells there for this purpose, so they would have fresh water for the journey home. Around a century later, the island was also settled by Loyalists after the American Revolutionary War.

And they never left. Which I suppose makes sense—if you've found paradise, why leave? As a result, the Bahamians on this island are almost entirely white. Over the centuries, the population stayed small, insular, and mostly made up of a few key families, such as the Pinders, the Higgs, the Sweetings, and the Alburys. Today, not much has changed—Spanish

71

Wells is home to fewer than two thousand people, known to be fiercely independent, and in some cases, conservative in their religious views.

In fact, when Hurricane Andrew wreaked havoc on this community in 1992, destroying shops, homes, and the only small hotel on the island, the religious community got involved. The church successfully petitioned that all liquor licenses should not be renewed. Thus, from 1992 to only a few years ago, Spanish Wells was a dry island. That's right—not a drop of alcohol. Not exactly a tourist magnet.

But like I said—tourism had never been on their radar to begin with.

Sure, Spanish Wells had gorgeous water, spectacular beaches, and a comfortable climate, like the rest of the Bahamas. Today, quaint cottages line a pristine coastline, interconnected by golf carts. Sounds idyllic, doesn't it? So how is it that this island community bucked the tourism trend? How have they prospered for hundreds of years in such relative isolation?

"Spanish Wells has the biggest spiny lobster and crawfish industry in the Bahamas," Bruce Pinder says. "We aren't a filthy rich island, but we are definitely a very comfortable island. You start off young, you go out to sea, and I mean, it is a great business, great income, so you are working half the year and the other half you can relax, or do side jobs, or anything like that."

Born in Nassau, Pinder's grandfather was from Spanish Wells. His grandmother was from Eleuthera. Although he spent his entire youth in the "big city," Pinder's parents would always take him to Spanish Wells for summers and long weekends. The connection never left him. Growing up, he knew the second he got out of high school where he was headed. And in 1999, at the age of eighteen, Pinder, bearing a true Spanish Wells name, packed up and left Nassau to seek his fortune in lobster fishing.

Funny enough, a very different animal would come to define him—but first, there would be more than a few twists and turns for young Pinder.

"I wasn't really the boating guy compared to my friends," he remembers.

"They were born and raised in the water. From as soon as they could swim, their parents would throw them overboard—go dive that conch, go get this and that. Having been born in Nassau, I went to the beach and all, and I could swim, but I was a little more wary of the open ocean."

This gut instinct would foreshadow things to come.

For years, Pinder worked as a fisherman. Then one day, while spearfishing out at sea, he found a promising spot. Fishermen on Spanish Wells use air compressors to reach the ocean floor. These air compressors sit there humming on the side of the boat, with a long plastic tube attached to it, running up to 250 feet. And at the end of it, there was Pinder, tube in his mouth, sling in his hands, gathering up as much fish and lobster as he could muster. However, above the surface, a storm was brewing.

In Pinder's words, "it just got a little complicated."

Fearing the storm, his fellow fisherman pulled him up too quickly. That was a huge mistake. When far below the surface, it's important for deep-sea divers to come up gradually. Failure to do so can result in decompression sickness, otherwise known as the bends. Due to the difference in pressure, deadly bubbles can form inside the body, resulting in severe joint pain, rashes, paralysis, and even death.

That's the technical version.

As Pinder put it: "As soon as I got out of the water, my elbow and knees on my right side felt like someone was pounding on them with a hammer. I had to be flown out on a helicopter to the United States and put in a decompression chamber."

This brush with death would keep Pinder out of the water—at least for a little while.

Pinder would still go out on lobster boats, but this time as the chef. Later, he would be recruited to help run a new private island development, known as Royal Island, not far from Eleuthera. But that didn't work out for long. The development went bust, and what's worse, Pinder had invested his savings in a ferry boat business, taking guests from the mainland of Eleuthera over to Royal Island. At twenty-three, he found himself heavily in debt.

But things got better. Pinder found ways to make money and pay off the debt. The couple moved to Abaco because he heard an island owned by Disney needed a ferry service. So he put that ferry boat to work. He also moonlighted as a bartender, rented golf carts, and even sold ice cream. He did everything he could to pay off that debt.

And it worked out—within a few years, Pinder's head was back above water. His wife became pregnant. And they decided to return to what always felt like home—Spanish Wells.

With a few dollars in his pocket, Pinder was mulling what to do next. He thought about opening a Subway or coffee shop on the island, but the population was so small. And tourists just didn't go there. After all, this was Spanish Wells. Before long, the sea was calling him. A friend was headed out lobster fishing, and one of the crew had dropped out. Pinder volunteered—but only to be the cook. Those memories of the bends were still fresh in his mind. Then, out at sea, one of his friends got an ear infection and couldn't dive.

Once again, Pinder volunteered.

"So I went off, and I wasn't out in the water for more than an hour, diving the lobster traps, when my lung collapsed," Pinder explains.

"Why? I hadn't done it in a long time. You're working hard underwater. You are breathing hard, working fast. When they pulled me from the water, I could barely breathe; my breathing was short and fast. It felt like my heart was going to give out. I didn't think I would make it to the hospital. I definitely thought I was going to die."

For the second time in his young life, Pinder was airlifted by helicopter, this time to Nassau, to perform emergency surgery. He remembers the complete exhaustion of trying to force enough oxygen in his lungs, hanging on for just a bit longer. His wife had recently given birth to their child, a baby girl.

"So all I did was kept picturing her," he says.

Pinder somehow pulled through that day. But diving was now a thing of the past—for good. Pinder had been born with lobster fishing in his blood. But fate was slowly moving him away from the luxurious lobster to the humble pig.

But the solution wasn't immediately obvious. With a wife and baby, what else does a young man do for a living on Spanish Wells?

In 2016, the swimming pig craze had also reached Eleuthera. Although Spanish Wells wasn't a tourism destination, this larger island to the South certainly was. Harbour Island, for example, has long been a high-end hotspot for affluent travelers seeking a quieter, more laid-back island lifestyle. Hotels, marinas, and rows of colorful homes, shops, and restaurants are navigated by golf cart. Perhaps the most famous landmark on the island is the Pink Sand Beach, which gets its color from an abundance of microscopic coral insects with red and pink shells. Sadly, Harbour Island and Eleuthera weren't known for swimming pigs. But that didn't stop droves of tourists from asking for it.

In stepped Thomas and Chuck Pinder—no relation to Bruce Pinder, although Bruce and Thomas were good friends. Like everyone else on Spanish Wells, Thomas and Chuck were lobster fisherman. But they also had a finger on the pulse.

As a side business, father and son decided to purchase a boat and offer charters to see Exuma's swimming pigs. And it worked—sort of. There was no doubt people wanted to see the pigs. There was just one problem—Eleuthera is more than 50 miles north of Pig Beach. The journey was long. And the price tag was higher, about $4,000 for the day, which was steep even for the affluent crowd of Harbour Island. It just wasn't scalable. So what did Thomas and Chuck do? Thomas went to speak with Uncle Marvin.

"Thomas's uncle, Uncle Marvin, is also my uncle, but not my real uncle. I'm just very close with the family. He owns an island just off Spanish Wells called Peek's Patch," (Bruce) Pinder recalls. "So Thomas and Chuck said to Uncle Marvin: 'Why don't we try and get some pigs, and put them on the island?'"

They took a page right out of the Peter Nicholson playbook in Exuma.

If distance is a problem, the solution is simple: bring them closer.

They're just pigs, after all.

Meeks Patch Island was just a small, uninhabited, yet beautiful island. With nothing to lose, and no other purpose for the island, Uncle Marvin agreed. If you can make something happen, make it happen, and we'll discuss it later, he said.

So Thomas and Chuck got going. They picked up some pigs from Eleuthera, a few more from Spanish Wells, and placed them on Meeks Patch. They built a pen. And like everyone else before them, they slowly encouraged the pigs to swim. Two months later, they were doing a few charters per week, but in Pinder's words: "They never really pushed it or advertised it. Spanish Wells is a fishing community. They know fishing. I knew I couldn't go fishing anymore. I've already had two helicopter rides. I wasn't going to have a third. I didn't think I could make it a third time."

Pinder did what any intelligent married man would do—he consulted his wife. He approached her with a plan to start a new business entirely focused on pigs. She was skeptical at first. Sure, the swimming pigs had become popular on other islands. But should we really throw

Meeks Patch Island, a previously uninhabited island just off Eleuthera and Spanish Wells, proved to be the perfect location for a new colony of swimming pigs. *Credit: Pig Beach Bahamas Tours @pigbeachbahamastours / IG.*

our life savings at . . . pigs? The family had managed to pull themselves out of debt once already. So his wife met him halfway.

"She didn't want me to go all in and invest too much money," Pinder says.

"So I went to my best friend, Janssen Perry. Funny enough, he was the one who convinced me to go fishing the last time, when I got the collapsed lung. I went to him and told him my plan. Turns out, he wanted to get out of fishing, too. He was getting older, and it was getting harder, and he wanted to spend more time at home with his family. Perry then turned to me and said: 'You want the check now?' And that's how it all started."

Pinder cashed that check, threw in his own investment, and bought a twenty-four-foot boat with a single engine so he could start running tours. Then he did something nobody else in Spanish Wells had ever done: he advertised. Pinder designed a logo, made signs, and peppered the roads throughout Eleuthera—Da Salty Pig was born. He started Facebook, Instagram, and Twitter accounts. He went out with his GoPro and camera to take stunning imagery of the area, and of course, of the pigs.

And finally, Pinder engaged hotels and second home rentals on Eleuthera and Harbour Island to recommend Da Salty Pig for all of their swimming pig needs.

He saw results almost immediately. In some cases, it was more than an hour drive up the spine of Eleuthera to reach the top, where Da Salty Pig would pick them up. But they came. Pinder suddenly had more tourists than he could handle. Within a few months, Perry and Pinder would purchase a new boat—a larger thirty-one-footer with twin engines. Soon afterwards, he sold that first boat they bought and got an even bigger one.

Pinder had finally found his calling—pigs.

For the first time, Da Salty Pig bought a full-service tourism product to Spanish Wells, a quiet island traditionally dominated by lobster fishermen. *Credit: Pig Beach Bahamas Tours, @pigbeachbahamastours / IG.*

"It's a real industry now. It's huge," he explains. "It is definitely the number-one attraction. I mean, really, with my life, my ups and downs, the pigs have meant a lot to me. I saw a dream and made it happen."

When Pinder first started, there were five charter boat companies in Eleuthera and Spanish Wells. Today, there are dozens of boats running tours, Pinder says. In 2020, he would further add to that total by founding yet another company, Pig Beach Bahamas Tours, after selling his share of Da Salty Pig to his friend and business partner, Janssen Perry. Apparently, there is more than enough swimming pig business to go around in Spanish Wells.

As for Thomas, Chuck, and Uncle Marvin?

With the huge influx of tourists to Meeks Patch, the group came up with an innovative system—they charged each guest, per head, to step

Since March 2016, Harbour Safaris, the only tour company operating out of Nassau that offers trips to see the pigs, has tripled the size of its fleet to accommodate demand. *Credit: Harbour Safaris, Nassau / @harboursafaris IG.*

foot on the island. Pinder simply added ten dollars to each guest booking. The result? The swimming pigs would now have an ample food and water supply—apart from what tourists already give them. They even hired a full-time custodian to look after the animals, rake the beach, and provide general maintenance for the attraction.

And it made sense. Like Pinder said, it's an industry now in Spanish Wells, a place where tourism didn't exist.

Indeed, everywhere I looked in the Bahamas, the swimming pigs were making their mark. Placing pigs on an island, and encouraging them to swim, seemed akin to sprinkling fairy dust. It worked like magic.

Of course, the biggest demand, by far, came from Nassau, where the vast majority of tourists travel. A tour company for the pigs soon emerged, almost by accident. Harbour Safaris never intended to run regular tours all the way to Exuma. One day, a client specifically requested a tour all the way to Pig Beach.

"It was a gorgeous day and we ended up with a lot of our initial promotional photos including Exuma and the swimming pigs," says Joanne Robertson, director of operations.

"This generated excitement through our website inquiries. So we put together an itinerary and began adding swimming pig excursions to our booking calendar, slowly at first, to gauge demand."

By March 2016, Harbour Safaris entered the swimming pig business in a big way. Ever since, they've been playing catch-up with the overwhelming demand.

The company has tripled the size of its fleet and runs tours several times a week, filling speedboats, literally strapping guests into their seats, and zooming more than eighty miles across the sea to the original Pig Beach in Exuma to catch a glimpse of the elusive swimming pig.

"We've had a number of pig enthusiasts on board. We've celebrated countless birthdays, and we've even assisted in a few proposals," Robertson adds.

A few years ago, Powerboat Adventures was the only company operating tours from Nassau. Today, there are dozens of boats leaving the nation's capital each day, all headed for the swimming pigs. *Credit: Powerboat Adventures.*

"One of the most memorable moments has got to be when one passenger dressed up in a full pig onesie at the beach to pose with the famed animals. That is some real piggy love right there."

It didn't take long for other tour boat operators to take notice.

Nigel Bowe, the founder of Powerboat Adventures, had been in the tour business since 1989—but he never gave much thought to swimming pigs.

Back then, the Thunderball Grotto, where they filmed the original James Bond film, was the big attraction. Bowe would take clients into the Exumas, see the Grotto and a few other sites, and maybe have an idyllic picnic on a beach.

And the business did well. But over time, Bowe started to think bigger. He realized he needed a base of operations in the Exumas to take his business to the next level. So in 1993, he approached the government of the day on acquiring an island known as Ship Channel Cay, located in northern Exuma, just thirty miles or so from Nassau. There, he could offer a "rustic glamping affair"—shark feeding, stingray encounters, snorkeling, a buffet lunch, toilets, and nature walks. The plan worked perfectly. When it came to tour boats out of Nassau, Bowe was the big game in town. He was a pioneer. And nobody else would offer a day trip to Exuma from Nassau for another twenty years.

And then came along Harbour Safaris.

"Nobody was doing it out of Nassau until about three years ago or so," Bowe explains. "Harbour Safaris did the first one, almost by accident, because the people demanded it. All of a sudden, we start getting calls. People ask: 'Do you go to the swimming pigs?' We'd tell them 'no, but we have this . . .' and the phone would go click."

Bowe realized he had to tweak his tour—or be left behind.

Fortunately for him, he had an advantage. Bowe was indeed wise to acquire an island way back in 1993. Big Major Cay was much further down the Exuma chain of islands, about eighty miles away from Nassau,

Ship Channel Cay, purchased by Nigel Bowe in the early nineties, turned out to be a wise investment. Rather than travel more than eighty miles in Big Major Cay, Ship Channel Cay, also in Exuma, was repurposed to offer swimming pigs, while only being half the distance from Nassau. *Credit: Powerboat Adventures.*

which is around double the distance of Ship Channel Cay. Here, Bowe had a much more accessible foothold—and the building blocks of yet another swimming pig attraction in the Bahamas.

The transition almost felt natural, according to Bowe. As it turns out, this would not be his first brush with pigs on Ship Channel Cay.

"Originally, in 1990, we had a feral wild boar that was quite tame," he remembers.

"Occasionally, he would come down and swim and look for food among the tourists. He caused a bit of a sensation to some people, and other people ignored him. Keep in mind, he was a wild boar, so he was a big, furry fellow. They are shorter and more wiry than domestic pigs, because they are searching for their own food.

"He had tusks, a much longer nose, and the hairs were pointier than domestic pigs. He also had slightly wider ears, almost like cat ears. Eventually he passed away after seventeen years. Stones lived his lifetime with us."

Stones? That's an unusual name for a pig.

"Well, years ago, in the old days, there were a lot of drugs coming through Exuma and onto the beach," Bowe says.

"One month, we were down there, and a load of marijuana washes up on the shoreline, and Stones, well he had taken a shine to it and actually ate a lot of the hemp. So, as you might imagine, he was stumbling quite happily all over the place after that. So we named him Stones."

A stoned swimming pig? In this case, a wild boar? Just when I thought the story of the swimming pigs couldn't get any more unusual, it does. Bowe and his family didn't know it at the time, but Stones would just be a taste of things to come. I wonder—were swimming pigs and the Bahamas simply meant to be?

Stones's unusual namesake aside, Bowe's story was a familiar one.

Whether it was Captain Jerry, local historian Cordell Thompson, the people of Staniel Cay, or just about any Bahamian that has seen a few years, they all told me the same thing: there have been animals on these islands—and in particular—pigs, for hundreds, if not thousands of years. If you were a Spanish or British sailor, what better animal to leave on islands than the pig? They're able to survive, adapt, and multiply. And a few generations later, they will go feral, just like Bowe's good friend Stones.

There were many feral pigs on Ship Channel Cay, Bowe explains. But Stones was special. For whatever reason, he was the tamest and interacted well with the guests. More than a few times, Bowe says, staff had to chase off other feral pigs that weren't quite so docile. Some of them even

Stones, a feral wild boar on Ship Channel Cay with an affinity for the ocean, was a curiosity for customers of Powerboat Adventures since the 1990s. Little did they know this pig would foreshadow the swimming pig craze to come. *Credit: Powerboat Adventures.*

had even larger tusks, which intimidated the guests and "wasn't good for business."

So bringing in a few domestic pigs? That would be a piece of cake.

Bowe had a friend who was a pig farmer down in Long Island, just south of Exuma. He bought three pigs from there, and then purchased another three, a different breed, in Nassau. By interbreeding, Bowe says he was able to produce a stronger, more genetically robust colony of pigs.

It didn't take long for the results to roll in. Powerboat Adventures was already the veteran in the Nassau tour boat scene. This "top dog" in the market already had the boats, nearly two dozen employees, and of course, Ship Channel Cay. Nevertheless, like everyone else in the country, swimming pigs changed his business.

According to Bowe, Powerboat Adventures is currently operating "the biggest boat in town"—60-foot jet boat, 2,000 horsepower, capable of transporting 70 people in one go. That's in addition to two other 40-footers, which the company tends to reserve for VIPs.

"We get a lot of VIPs . . . people that fly their jets down and want to swim with the pigs. And they want a boat all to themselves," he says.

"It is all really based on Instagram, Facebook, and social media. Your production with Charlie Smith put it on the map, there are no two ways about it. But once it got going, there was so much demand, but little supply. So everyone got in the supply business."

For Bowe, things have changed since 1989. Back then, he remembers having to create a market. It took him two years to gain enough tourists to buy a second boat. Today, Bowe sees tour operators everywhere— what he terms "jump up and go." There are now six individual operators working out of Nassau, all focused on the pigs. That's around twenty-five boats, Bowe says, running nearly every day from the nation's capital.

"It has changed the tourism dynamic. I mean, it has made a remarkable difference to our bottom line. And generally, it has been a great stimulus for the country. It's bizarre. It's weird. And it has absolutely superseded every other attraction in the Bahamas."

The fact that the original Pig Beach was located in Exuma didn't seem to matter anymore—the people wanted swimming pigs, and they were willing to do whatever it takes to see them.

Sometimes, because of bad weather or lack of space, I had to deal with crushed tourists in Nassau who wouldn't get to swim with the pigs. Desperate, they would often board a plane, fly to Exuma, head out on the boat, and fly back to Nassau, all in the same day. At first, it started off as private charters. But it wasn't long before planes placed images of swimming pigs on their tails. Flamingo Air, one of the local airlines, started offering daily service to Staniel Cay, advertising to its customers: "The only airline that takes you directly to the swimming pigs."

But nobody was missing out more than those arriving on a cruise ship. According to official statistics from Bahamian government, of the 7.2 million or so people that flocked to this archipelago in 2019, a staggering 5.4 million passed through on a cruise.

Cruise ship passengers would be crushed when I told them: I'm sorry, it is a full day tour over to Exuma. There isn't enough time to see the pigs.

And even if there was enough time, it was always a risk for tour boat operators to get the passengers back in time. Plus, there was always the weather problem—because it was a long trip over the open ocean to reach Exuma from Nassau, cancellations happened all the time if winds were a bit too gusty. These realities created an opportunity for yet another player to join the swimming pig party.

In stepped Treasure Island, a perfectly situated cay in the Berry Islands, directly in the path of the cruise ship companies.

For them, serving cruise ship passengers was nothing new. Like Bowe, tours existed well before the pigs. Each cruise ship company had their own little island paradise for their guests. Norwegian Cruise Lines had Great Stirrup Cay; Royal Caribbean had Coco Cay. And for years, Treasure Island, right around the corner, offered "Stingray City," where guests could get right in the water with these creatures.

"It was just a rock," Brandon Honkofsky says, CEO of Treasure Island.

Back then, the rock was known as Goat Cay. And when Honofsky says a rock, he means a rock. Previously, tourists from the cruise ships would pull up to a floating dock anchored on the seabed. People would hop out and interact with the stingrays. And that was it—there was no infrastructure.

But when the pigs came on the scene, everything changed.

"We had to build a beach, loading docks, electricity, water, and we had to purchase the pigs and raise them," Honkofsky explains.

"That was what really drove all the infrastructure—the pigs. That's the big ticket. We saw the demand, and really, the stingrays didn't compare. All of a sudden, we are building a bar, an observation deck, a washing area and a food area. . . . It was a whole transformation around the pigs."

All told, Honkofsky says it cost millions to transform what used to be a barren island known as Goat Cay, to what effectively became a bustling new Pig Island.

Goat Cay? Pig Island? No competition, right?

But wait—companies are spending millions to transform private islands? And places that never even thought about tourism, like Spanish Wells, are now all about the pigs? Over time, it really started to dawn on me—these swimming pigs are not only a good bit of fun. They are transforming lives.

Take Babara Darville, the owner of Celerity Eco Adventures, in Grand Bahama. This island, the northernmost in the chain, has often been referred to as the Bahamas "second city." In addition to shipyards and other industries, Grand Bahama has hotels as well as being a convenient stop for cruise ships.

For Darville, that had always been her bread and butter—catering to these tourists, particularly those stopping by on a cruise. She operated a restaurant and bar and provided snorkeling and kayaking.

"When people would come to Grand Bahama, they would usually ask—'Where are the swimming pigs? We want to swim with the pigs.' They just wouldn't understand why we don't have them," she recalls. "So hey, that gave me an idea."

And like everyone else, the pigs changed everything.

"Oh my god . . . they have caused my business to go from, I'd say a 10 to a 100," she explains. "It has really been exhilarating. And you know what I tell my staff when we have meetings? I say: 'Listen, they aren't coming to see you. They are coming to see the pigs.' I mean, it seems as though it is one of the main reasons they come to the island. People say: 'We only came to see the pigs.'"

Because Grand Bahama is close to Florida, Balearia Caribbean can bring tourists from Miami and Fort Lauderdale for the day, she says.

"And we have people from Russia, France, all over . . . Australia. They've all heard about them and want to come see these famous swimming pigs," Darville adds.

Listening to Darville got me thinking even further. How many Bahamians were now linked with these pigs? How many employees? And not just the people who directly work for these pig colonies. There are tour boats, hotels, restaurants, and taxi drivers. How many livelihoods? How many families?

Dionisio D'Aguilar, the Minister of Tourism for The Bahamas, sums it up best.

"It is remarkably significant that these swimming pigs have had the economic impact they've had. I mean, we can't thank them enough—we should give them all knighthoods," he chuckles.

All kidding aside—he is absolutely correct.

In a few short years, the swimming pigs became the darlings of Bahamian tourism. They knew no borders. From Abaco, to Eleuthera and Spanish Wells, to Long Island, to Ship Channel Cay, to Treasure Island, to Rose Island in Nassau, to Grand Bahama, the pigs were no longer an attraction in only Exuma.

They became a national attraction, a national treasure, even. In a country defined by tourism, the pigs didn't just change Exuma. They changed the Bahamas.

Quality Time with the Swimming Pigs of Exuma

Credit: Edward Lowe, Enlphotography, @enlphotography / IG.

Credit: Howie Sonnenschein.

Credit: Howie Sonnenschein.

Credit: T. R. Todd.

Credit: T. R. Todd.

Credit: T. R. Todd.

Credit: T. R. Todd.

Credit: T. R. Todd.

Credit: T. R. Todd.

Credit: T. R. Todd.

Credit: T. R. Todd.

Credit: T. R. Todd.

Credit: T. R. Todd.

Credit: T. R. Todd.

Credit: T. R. Todd.

Credit: T. R. Todd.

Credit: Amy Thorne, @peaks_to_ports / IG.

Credit: Amy Thorn, @peaks_to_ports / IG.

Credit: Cate Biggs, @thebiggsisland / IG.

Credit: André Musgrove, @andremusgrove / IG.

Credit: Anthony Miaoulis, @miaoulis17 / IG.

Credit: Brenden Butler, @brendan_butler / IG.

Credit: Elona Karafin, @elonatheexplorer / IG.

Credit: Forrest Galante, @forrest.galante / IG.

Credit: Jenny Yanyuk, @jennifermartyn / IG.

Credit: Impulse Yacht, @impulseyacht / IG.

Credit: Jakob Owens, @jakobowens / IG.

Credit: Jakob Owens, @jakobowens / IG.

Credit: Jay Namoc, @haejaen / IG.

Credit: Jyotsna Shankar, @jyo_shankar / IG.

Credit: Kaloipe, @kaloipe / IG.

Credit: Max Strong, @maxstrong / IG.

Credit: Michael Morrow, @gumballteamanime / IG.

Credit: Molly Golden, @goldengirltravel / IG.

Credit: Morgan Potochnic, @morggselizabeth / IG.

Credit: Nicoleta Milkowski, @nicoletanomer / IG.

Credit: Sara Haglund, @sara.haglund / IG.

Credit: Sonia Rockwell, @soniarockwell / IG.

Credit: Tomie Kimura.

Courtesy of Wanda Lee Tran, photo by Adam Opris Photography @adamoprisphotography / IG.

Credit: Zach Stadler, @zachstadler / IG.

Credit: Peter Pontone, @petepontone / IG.

Credit: Gabriela Rodriguez, @bahamasphotographer / IG.

Credit: Amanda Bukobza,
@amandabukobza / IG.

Credit: Ellie M. Zee, @elliemzee / IG.

Credit: Arianny Celeste & Taylor King, @ariannycelest & @theking_/ IG.

Credit: Ellie M. Zee, @elliemzee / IG.

Credit: Erin Muñoz, @erinmunozmusic / IG.

Credit: Makenna Villamor, @makenna_villamor / IG.

Credit: Fefa Caram, @fefacaram / IG.

Credit: Jamie Villamor @jamie_villamor / IG.

Credit: Jamie Villamor @jamie_villamor / IG.

Credit: Jeffrey Zausch, @jeffzausch (photo by @erinmunozmusic) / IG.

Credit: Gil Antolin, @luxuryworldtraveler / IG.

Credit: Laney Heard, @martinis2miles / IG.

Credit: Kate Boxler, @katieboxler / IG.

Credit: Kate Boxler, @katieboxler / IG.

Credit: Cesar Wataya, @mochilacheia / IG.

Credit: Tony Carvajal, @tonycarvajal_ (photo by @hmgriff11) / IG.

Credit: Austin Gallagher, @draustingallagher / IG.

Credit: Pig Beach Bahamas Tours, @pigbeachbahamastours / IG.

Credit: Kimberly Boldon, @kimberlyellen1106 / IG.

CHAPTER 4
That's Some Pig

At the beginning of *Charlotte's Web*, the classic 1952 children's novel by E.B. White, Fern asks her mother where her father, Mr. Arable, is going carrying that axe.

"Out to the hoghouse," replies Mrs. Arable. "Some pigs were born last night."

Mr. Arable plans to kill the runt of the litter—small and weak—because it won't amount to anything and will probably die anyway.

Fern begs and pleads with her father not to kill the runt.

A tearful Fern, grasping her father's axe, wonders if she had been born weak and small whether she would have been killed, too? Her father of course dismisses such a ridiculous statement—you are a girl, and that runt is just a pig.

"I see no difference," replies Fern, still hanging on to the ax. "This is the most terrible case of injustice I ever heard of."

Her father, noticeably moved, gives in to his daughter's plea. She will have to look after the piglet now, to see how difficult a runt can be.

And where does the triumphant Fern return to?

The farmhouse's breakfast table, and the smell of bacon.

This opening scene from the best-selling children's book of all time displays our rather complicated relationship with pigs. The author is playing with the notion of what we consider to be valuable life—and no animal seems to generate an emotional response quite like the cute runt of the litter, who would soon be named Wilbur.

As a society, we have an exceptional affinity for the pig. Piglet, Porky Pig, the Three Little Pigs, Miss Piggy: these are all beloved characters, harking back to our innocence as children.

And who doesn't love Babe?

This adorable orphaned pig wants to be a sheepdog and miraculously wins the county fair for Hoggett, the farmer. Only the intelligent pig could communicate and lead the mindless sheep through the obstacle course, followed by the famous line by the proud Hoggett: "That'll do pig. That'll do."

The feature film made more than $250 million at the box office, won best picture at the Golden Globes in 1995, and was nominated for seven Academy Awards.

We love a comeback story, don't we?

We root for the underdog, or in this case, the "underpig." What about an "undercow"? "Underchicken"? It doesn't have the same ring to it.

How could Hoggett butcher such an animal, with such intelligence? Such charisma?

Wilbur, the runt, is no slouch, either.

In the "miracle" scene of *Charlotte's Web*, Charlotte, the spider, in an effort to save Wilbur's life, spends the night weaving the words "Some Pig!" into her web above the pig's pen. When the humans discover it, Wilbur and Charlotte become famous, once again blurring the lines of what is considered just an animal, and what is thought of as intelligent life. Wilbur's life is spared.

Colleen Glenney Boggs, a professor of English at Dartmouth College, argues that Charlotte's message in the web is a direct echo back to the opening scene of the book, when the mother tells Fern that Mr. Arable is off to kill "some pigs."

Boggs says Charlotte's message "transforms dispensable life into exceptional life."

Is the pig really so exceptional?

Yale certainly seemed to think so, when it hosted an expansive conference in 2015 entitled "Pig Out" that examined the role of pigs in society. For an entire weekend, the Yale Program of Agrarian Studies, Duke University Women's Studies Program, and the Yale Sustainable Food Program held lectures and invited debate. The conference ran the gambit of history, agriculture, literature, and religious significance.

All of this scholarship for . . . the pig?

How is it that Fern could emphatically save Wilbur's life and then stroll back to the breakfast table for some crispy bacon?

I suppose, in a way, her actions are pretty straightforward. Because, honestly, who doesn't love bacon?

Pigs are both delicious and adorable, right?

But let's drill down a little bit further—is there more to this pig than meets the eye? On one hand, we cast them as heroes, comedians, and companions. We become attached to them as children. And on the other, not only do we eat them, but we also use these animals as the butt of jokes, or to degrade others.

And when was the last time you called someone a pig?

If you did, odds are you were saying the person was dirty, disgusting, greedy, gluttonous, or lazy. What do you say when someone or something isn't as good as it looks? You put "lipstick on a pig." If someone or something is "hog wild"? Completely out of control. In the UK, "a pig in a poke" means you've been cheated and didn't properly check something out before buying it. In India, they have a saying: "What does a pig know about the scent of rose water?" Yet another insult, meaning only beautiful things can be appreciated by beautiful people. Indeed, "pearls before swine," grounded in Christian biblical history as part of Jesus's Sermon on the Mount, follows a very similar theme: giving something valuable to those who don't appreciate it.

In Afrikaans, a language spoken in South Africa, the expression "to be the pig in the tale" of course means something very basic—to be the villain.

And if something is just flat-out impossible? Sure, that'll happen— "when pigs fly."

So why do we build up iconic characters like Wilbur and Babe? Why are they lovable, intelligent, sensitive heroes one minute, and filthy, unworthy villains the next?

Whatever happened to our beloved childhood characters?

This sociological schizophrenia toward pigs can be seen most of all in two of the world's biggest religions—Islam and Judaism.

"The pig is a taboo animal," says Walid Saleh, an associate professor in the Department for the Study of Religion at the University of Toronto.

As a scholar of the Qur'an, he explains that it's quite clear pork isn't on the menu for Muslims—even touching or being in proximity to the animal is considered vile. But Saleh tells me that it's difficult to pin down an exact reason for this complete revulsion; pigs have always been perceived as unclean scavengers. He even openly questioned the practical reasoning behind this bias in today's modern world.

"We don't know why, given that the pig is one of the most prolific animals as a domestic animal," he adds. "It could be of immense help to smaller families. You could raise it in small domestic environments. So, in a sense, it is very counterintuitive as to why a culture would not decide to have a pig."

Meanwhile, speaking at Yale's Pig Out conference in 2015, entrepreneur and food writer Jeffrey Yoskowitz shed some light on the "underground pork economy" in Israel.

He detailed the laws enacted in Israel in the 1950s and '60s that banned the raising of pigs and the selling of pork, except in special regions where Christians and Arabs lived. Yoskowitz displayed pictures of protests in 1989, as secular Jews and Orthodox Jews clashed over the sale and consumption of pork. These acts of defiance, he explained, were less about the pig and more about "a litmus test for democracy," or a rallying point for more secular Jews—a symbol of liberation and freedom.

Liberation and freedom? Democracy?

For the humble pig, this is pretty heavy stuff.

After he arrived in Tel Aviv in 2007 to work on a pig farm and investigate the topic, Yoskowitz described the multiple arson attacks on shops selling pork by Orthodox Jews, even after the state abolished the ban on pork in the early 1990s.

Today, Jews in Israel, even those who eat pork, will often choose to not say "*chazir*," the Hebrew word for pig, but rather speak of it in code. "White steak," "short cow," or "the other thing,": these are the euphemisms Israelis use to describe pork, Yoskowitz explained.

"It shows as much as you can reject this idea of abstaining from pork, you still internalize it," he told the conference attendees.

So is pork the Voldemort of foods? The pig that shall not be named?

I knew at this point that we were dealing with a more complex issue than delicious and adorable. So I kept digging. I discovered just how much Yoskowitz had done to pull back the curtain on pigs in Jewish life.

He is also the founder of the website Pork Memoirs, where Jews offer short essays about their relationship with the complicated meat.

One entry states: "My bacon cherry popped, I don't think I can go back to a life without the forbidden fruit (baby back ribs count toward my three-to-five servings a day, right?). I'm not sure my children will grow up in a kosher home like I did, but I think that's okay. They say religiosity skips a generation. The same cannot be said, however, for baconlust."

Another confesses: "When I quit keeping kosher, I quit hard. I ate everything I could remember eating before I declared treyf off limits. Except, peculiarly enough, for that particular bacon cheeseburger. Truthfully, I'm afraid to eat it, the way you might be afraid to see someone very dear to you whom you haven't seen for years. What if it's not the way I remember it? Or worse, what if it's exactly how I remember it? And there I am, sitting on a plastic bench in a mall in the middle of somewhere, sobbing like a toddler."

As it turns out, Yoskowitz started the website in response to the passionate responses he received from both Jews and Muslims during his research in Israel.

"I was going all around Israel and the West Bank, meeting Israelis, Palestinians, Arabs, Americans, and Europeans. Everyone, whether they were religious or not, they laughed and told their stories about the time they almost ate pork accidentally, or the time they ate pork," he later explained to me.

"They all wanted to tell me their interaction with these animals. Like someone who had grown up kosher and lived in a kibbutz, and accidentally tasted prosciutto, and for some reason it tasted like lox to them, which they missed from New York. So they would go to the back of the kibbutz store to order the prosciutto because it reminded them of their Jewish New York culture. Little things like that just blew me away, and I wanted to create a website and invite people to share their stories with me."

But why pigs? Why would Yoskowitz be so interested in this topic at all?

The grandchild of holocaust survivors, Yoskowitz said the family was not particularly religious. He went to synagogue only until his bar mitzvah. But he grew up in a kosher home, and as he got older, Yoskowitz noticed that keeping kosher was always really important. His grandmother told him stories of fleeing to a remote village in Siberia during the Second World War. At various times, she and her family were offered pork, and even though they were starving, she would say no.

"It was an assertion of their cultural and religious identities," he says. "Even in the face of hunger and death."

His grandfather was in a prison in Siberia, one of Stalin's camps. And when he survived the war and came to the United States, the second job he got, which he held for thirty-three years, was as a hand-boner in a pig processing plant. He never ate the pork, even though one of the few benefits of working at the plant was free hams.

He took the hams but gave them to his neighbors as a gift.

Jordan Rosenblum, an associate professor of classical Judaism at the University of Wisconsin-Madison, openly told me he eats pork, but "I'm very careful in the types I eat." Overall, he has nothing against dining on swine, saying the animal was given a "bad rap," and "they are not as dirty as people think."

According to the Hebrew Bible, animals that are permissible to eat are domesticated quadrupeds that have split hooves and chew the cud. That is, animals that regurgitate food from the stomach to the mouth so that they can chew it a second time. Pigs, like humans, have a single-chamber stomach, whereas cows and sheep, for example, have four-chamber stomachs. Sheep and cows chew the cud and have four-chamber stomachs for many reasons, one being that they eat mostly grass. Pigs and humans have a less complicated process to digest food.

It's immediately obvious that a cow or a sheep fulfills both requirements to make the animal "kosher."

A pig is not so simple—you'd have to cut it open to find out.

Although the Hebrew Bible might explain why Jews have traditionally avoided pigs, Rosenblum argues that the issue is more complex.

"In the Roman diet, for example, they loved the pig," he explains.

"So for Jews, around two thousand years ago, it became the most commonly interacted-with animal that was not kosher. It came to represent Jewishness and non-Jewishness. It became an identity marker, or a cultural signifier. Can you be Roman if you don't eat a pig? Why would you not eat a pig? Pigs are delicious. It is irrational to do that. So if you choose not to do that, you must be irrational."

On the flip side, to not eat pork became an identity marker of Judaism.

"The pig looks kosher," Rosenblum argues, "but when you cut it up, you realize it doesn't chew the cud. And that's exactly the problem with Rome. Rome looks just fine from the outside, but if you look inside it, it's corrupt. Overall, the pig is a great way to compare rhetoric of identity around a single object both groups were talking about. It became a convenient way to talk about other issues. I see the pig as having more than two thousand years of symbolic value."

Could this historical baggage be a source of its sociological complexity today? Maybe deep down, we know there is more to a pig than an oink.

The scientific community certainly thinks so.

For many years, the Kimmela Center for Animal Advocacy has taken a passionate yet scientific approach to the fight for animal rights, with the goal of turning exploitation into respect. The organization brands itself as a kind of bridge between conventional animal rights advocacy, based on emotion, life choices, and morality, and the actual science behind the animal kingdom.

Not surprisingly, the Center is particularly interested in pigs.

Not only do scientists consider pigs intelligent, but when it comes to their cognition and social and emotional complexity, they are right up there with primates.

But wait a minute—similar to primates? Aren't primates considered our closest ancestor? Where does that leave the pig?

It has long been observed that pig organs are similar to those in humans.

So similar, in fact, that in January 2017, scientists announced that they had created the first successful human–animal hybrids—with the pig as the host. Although controversial for many, the experiment, involving nearly 186 living embryos, proved once and for all that human cells can be incorporated into and even grown inside a pig. The findings were reported in the scientific journal *Cell* by an international team of researchers, led by the Salk Institute for Biological Studies in La Jolla, California.

According to a recent article on this topic in *National Geographic*, a new person is added to the national waiting list for organ transplants in the United States every ten minutes; twenty-two people on the list will die, every day.

Researchers hope that a successful human-animal hybrid program could have a major impact on cutting down these wait times and saving lives. In the future, could humans have access to an unlimited stockpile of replacement organs, grown inside pigs?

Would people even want that?

For scientists such as those at the Kimmela Center for Animal Advocacy, pigs are celebrated for their cognitive similarities to humans, not for their organs.

In a 2015 white paper entitled "Thinking Pigs: Cognition, Emotion, and Personality," researchers reviewed a series of studies showing pigs are capable of excellent long-term memory. They also understand symbolic language, have a sense of time, play creatively, have complex social communities, and easily distinguish other individuals (both pigs and humans).

In one study, researchers pit two pigs against each other in a competitive battle for food. Except one of the pigs was given a wee bit of an advantage—it knew where the food had been hidden. So what did the uninformed pig do? It learned to follow the pig-in-the-know to the food source and swiped the meal first.

In subsequent tests, the informed pigs learned to outwit the uninformed pigs to avoid being followed and then sped up their foraging to beat out their competitors before they realized the jig was up.

In another study, researchers asked the pigs to choose between two humans—one who was ignoring them and another who was being attentive. Every time, the pig picked the human who showed interest.

"The body of findings on pigs' perspective taking, sensitivity to attention state and social presence shows that they belong in a group of very sophisticated animals, such as great apes, ravens, and dolphins, all of whom possess a keen and nuanced understanding of their role in their social group," the study states.

The more I looked into it, the more I found about pigs and their similarities to humans.

A 2016 study by the University of Lincoln, published in *Biology Letters*, found that pigs can be either pessimists or optimists, just like humans, and there is a way to measure this. Using thirty-six pigs, researchers gave some of them a cushy lifestyle, with plenty of room to move around and a large straw bed. The others received a much smaller space with much less straw.

All the pigs were then given access to food in the same circumstances. In a room, there was one bowl filled with enticing chocolate treats and another with unappetizing coffee beans. When a third bowl was later introduced, sometimes with chocolate, sometimes with coffee, those pigs with a less-fortunate lifestyle were far more likely to not give the new bowl a try. In other words, the scientists claimed it was the first time cognitive bias had been investigated in nonhuman animals.

Meanwhile, a recent study in the journal *Nature* claimed to have conducted the largest-ever investigation into the pig genome. It determined that pigs suffer from the same genetic and protein malfunctions that result in many human diseases and conditions, such as Alzheimer's, Parkinson's, and obesity.

Swine were found to be adaptable, easy to seduce with food, and susceptible to domestication—not unlike people.

So what does this mean for the swimming pigs?

These studies do explain a lot. Pigs have clear intelligence and willingly engage people; they have character traits and complexities that we find interesting.

But is that the whole answer?

There is no doubt the swimming pigs of Exuma are totally original. They defy expectation. And for sure, they rocketed to this level of popularity on the back of the Internet, through countless social media posts, selfies, and hashtags, feeding into our desire to share, to be seen, to be envied, to be followed.

But there has to be more to it.

In the classic political satire *Animal Farm*, George Orwell imagines Manor Farm as being ruled by pigs. Old Major, Napoleon, Snowball, Squealer, Minimus, and Pinkeye, among a few others, jostle for power and control among the farmers and other animals. Although the novel is generally thought to satirize the Russian Revolution of 1917, and the rise of Stalin (represented by Napoleon) and the Soviet Union, it is also a more general critique of the nature of power, the perversion of politics, the effectiveness of propaganda, and the manipulation of the masses.

The pigs initially lay down the rules—the Seven Commandments—saying, for example, that anyone who walks on two legs is the enemy, no animal shall sleep in a bed, no animal shall drink alcohol, and all animals are equal. Over time, as the pigs gain power, they start to act more like humans, by drinking alcohol and sleeping on beds. They begin to walk upright, carry whips, and wear clothes. As time goes on, the "rules" of the farm shift to accommodate those in power, and eventually, by the end of the novel, the so-called Seven Commandments are erased with a single phrase: "All animals are equal but some animals are more equal than others."

Napoleon holds a party for everyone on the farm, and as the animals look between the humans and pigs, they can no longer tell the difference.

In all the pigs' sensitivity, in all their intelligence, curiosity, personality, and genetic similarities, in their intimate presence in our culture and religion, I wonder if the true magic of the swimming pigs of Exuma, the real reason people flock to that perfect beach is because of some more profound connection.

In them, we see us.

When Joanne Lefson decided to start an animal sanctuary, the first animal she chose was a pig.

For Lefson, a native of South Africa, it was a natural choice: not only were pigs intelligent creatures, but they lived, in her words, in the most "horrendous conditions." So she visited a nearby slaughterhouse outside of Cape Town on a Sunday; she figured on the weekend the workers would be more relaxed.

Her strategy was simple—convince the workers to let her buy some pigs in a "normal, professional manner." She wasn't looking for trouble.

Fortunately, the workers, as anticipated, were in an easygoing mood. They were a bit perplexed, granted, as to why this middle-aged woman showed up to an industrial farm to purchase piglets, but nevertheless, she talked her way in. After all, they had plenty of inventory to spare.

The workers opened industrial steel doors to hundreds of squealing piglets.

"I went something like: 'Okay, go 'head, grab two,'" Lefson remembers.

"It was a slightly smaller factory farm, so I would say a couple hundred pigs per section. The mother was in a crate and in this other blocked-off concrete area where the piglets were running around, sliding around everywhere, and crap everywhere, as you can imagine. It was a quick in and out, just get the hell out of there.

"And basically they just scurried along this damn concrete depressing floor, and I had to get whomever I could get. They didn't know they were going to hoggy heaven. They were just trying to get away from this crazy person."

Lefson scooped up the first warm bodies that fell into her hands.

Talk about the lottery—of those two hundred or so piglets scampering away for dear life, 198 of them would soon be a bacon sandwich.

"The poor things stank. My car has never recovered, even though it has been ten months," she says.

It was October 2016 when those two lucky piglets, both females, stumbled out of the car and into their new life. From an enclosed, cold concrete room to wide-open, grassy fields, these pigs would form the bedrock of the new Farm Sanctuary SA.

But it wasn't Lefson's first foray into an animal rights campaign. Back in 2009, she sold everything, raised some money, and embarked on a world tour across five continents with her rescue dog, Oscar, to raise awareness for the millions of homeless dogs worldwide. Since she was a director of a dog adoption center, the move made sense to her, in her own way. As she visited thousands of doggy adoption centers worldwide, she peppered the Internet with artistic photos of her pup in front of some of the world's most recognizable landmarks, such as the Eiffel Tower and the Great Wall of China.

"How can you take him to China? People eat dogs in China," Lefson remembers some of her perplexed followers telling her. In 2011, she wrote an entire book about her world tour, titled *Ahound the World: My Travels With Oscar.*

For Lefson, being provocative and challenging the norm were exactly the point. Even then, with Oscar, she showed a nose for marketing, a flair for the dramatic, and an imagination to cast animals in a new and unusual light.

It was just the right training for what came next.

Back at the farm sanctuary, Lefson knew that pigs were smart animals and they would need to be entertained; there were some soccer and tennis balls lying around the yard. Surely, that would suffice?

Also on the property was a construction site, including some paintbrushes.

As fate would have it, one of the piglets, during one of its many wanderings, appeared especially enamored with a brush. Maybe it was the bristles the pig found interesting, Lefson thought. Pigs also have bristles, right? It was one of the few things she didn't want to eat, which Lefson found curious, considering this piglet wanted to eat everything.

Nope, instead, she simply held the brush in her mouth, as if with purpose.

Like a nurturing a parent, Lefson had an idea—she purchased some canvas and paint and left them outside the barn. It was time for an experiment. And to her amazement, Pigcasso, as she would soon be known, started painting.

"If she sees the brushes set up, she will simply walk over and paint," Lefson explains. Sometimes, I'll pick the colors for her. When I wake up in the morning, she sees me and gets totally excited. She starts singing. They should be making CDs of pigs singing, not just humpback whales. She wants to get into the studio and paint, and eat, and she will do that for half an hour, or an hour.

"Then perhaps she will pass out for a while. Suddenly, she will make noises again, and she is ready to paint and eat again. And she decides what she wants to do. She's big now—you can't make her do anything she doesn't want to do. But in principle, she loves to eat, sleep, and paint. Paint, sleep, and eat."

Much like the swimming pigs, Pigcasso, now a few hundred pounds heavier, has grown into an Internet sensation.

Lefson describes her as a "creative diva" who can be both loving and temperamental, so it is easy to understand why Pigcasso is so popular in the digital age of YouTube and social media. It is quite the head-scratcher to watch a giant pig oinking and grunting as it attacks a canvas, brush in mouth, with such zest and zeal.

146

Ever since she was a piglet, Pigcasso has shown an interest in painting. With paint, brushes, and an easel waiting, Pigcasso will paint something new every day without any encouragement or instruction. *Credit: Joanne Lefson.*

Pigcasso's work can be purchased online or right from his gallery at the farm. Lefson said his works have sold for thousands of dollars. She plans to hold the first-ever professional exhibition of art created entirely by an animal. *Credit: Joanne Lefson.*

It's exactly the kind of video, or image, that makes you want to share, comment, or like on social media, not so different from some other pigs I know.

And then you realize that Pigcasso, according to Farm Sanctuary SA, is selling works of art for as much as US$20,000. You can buy these original artworks—titled *Candy*, *Capitalism*, or *Flow*—at the farm or through the online shop.

Heck, you can even commission an original painting and get a video of the process to boot, with every work signed by Pigcasso's paint-dipped snout.

Sounds a bit out there? A bit out of "left field"? Lefson has heard it all.

Are you kidding me? It's just random scribbles on paper. The art doesn't really mean anything. How can an animal, intelligent or not, have its own art gallery? It's ridiculous. It's just an animal.

To the cynics, she says: "Pigcasso's work is a reflection of the completely spontaneous. She is an individual, interesting, intelligent being. And she is creative. She paints how she feels in that moment, getting rid of all the nonsense we overanalyze. We can't think of it as a certain way human beings would; she wouldn't paint an American flag, for example. She doesn't think of things our way. I think it is a lesson for all of us to be in the moment."

Remember that other piglet she saved?

Rosie didn't turn out to be quite so artistic. Instead, she is more the run-of-the-mill pig. Lefson refers to her as her little "monster," because she generally eats everything in sight, including paintbrushes.

"If I gave her a paint brush, she would swallow it whole. And burp," Lefson says.

The farm brought in another rescue pig recently, named Piggy Sue. Again, this particular swine hasn't shown an interest in or aptitude for art like Pigcasso, but Lefson still has some hope for this one.

For Lefson, the point is, like people, not all pigs are created equal. That Pigcasso has a talent, an interest, a quirk—whatever you wish to call it—is further proof.

Lefson now has various rescue animals on the farm: sheep, goats, cows.

Although Pigcasso, not surprisingly, remains the poster pig.

Lefson is dead serious in her ambitions; that is, among other things, to hold the first-ever professional exhibition of art created entirely by an animal, in Cape Town by the fall of 2017. All the proceeds from the art go toward keeping the farm sanctuary functional. It's through this method, Lefson believes, that society can make the connection between bacon and Pigcasso, that behind each meal is potentially a talented "individual."

"It is just a means to expose and to give the pig some air space, and to inspire people to think differently. That's really what it's all about," she explains.

Perhaps no other hog has done more to help people think differently, at least in North America, than Esther the Wonder Pig.

Derek and Steve, the proud parents of a five-hundred-pound pig, have inspired people around the world, not because Esther has a remarkable talent, such as painting, swimming, or juggling beach balls. Instead, they won people over through their generosity of spirit and dedication, and by allowing the personality of Esther to shine through.

Esther was misrepresented as a micro pig in the summer of 2012, when Steve purchased the four-pound piglet from a friend. By the time Esther had mushroomed in size, her dads had already decided on a new road in life, devoted to the respect, conservation, and advocacy of animals. With a massive crowdfunding campaign, Derek and Steve ultimately purchased a farm in the relatively nondescript town of Campbellville, Ontario, and later renamed it the Happily Ever Esther Farm Sanctuary. Today, the farm is home to all kinds of rescued animals. Derek and Steve have appeared in countless articles and television programs and recently published the *New York Times* best-selling book *Esther the Wonder Pig: Changing the World One Heart at a Time.* In a sense, Esther has become an industry onto herself; Derek and Steve, along with the sanctuary's entire team, sell a whole line of merchandise, such as jewelry, autographed photos (with the snout, of course), hats, T-shirts, baby onesies, and pretty much everything in between.

Derek and Steve have even branched out into tourism; in 2017, they did their first-ever "Esther Cruise" through the Caribbean.

What made this possible, not so unlike with Pigcasso or the swimming pigs, is an army of social media followers. Every moment, every oink, every grunt of Esther's life, whether hamming around inside the home with Derek and Steve or out on the farmyard, is meticulously chronicled and shared with the outside world. For animal rights activists like Lefson, or Esther's dads, the twenty-first century offers an unprecedented opportunity to broadcast their message of equality for all living things.

Could the Internet be the great equalizer? Is this the golden age of animal advocacy? And will the pig, the evolution of Miss Piggy, be the head cheerleader?

Is it finally the pig's time to shine?

Esther's superpower is love. For Pigcasso, it's art. And for the swimming pigs ... well, it's swimming, the juxtaposition of the clearest, most beautiful water in the world with the animal society has traditionally viewed as dirty.

"Anytime we can help people interact with farm animals and reconnect with that empathy for farm animals is a real positive," Lefson says. "They are normally all hidden away, so I say the more, the better. If people in the Bahamas can go and pick up these pigs, and connect with them in a new way, people will have a reawakened connection with what we as a society are doing to these animals."

And the more I looked into it, the more I realized there were many stories of people pushing the envelope with pigs, sometimes in the most unexpected places.

In Kew, a suburban neighborhood in Greater London, Olivia Mikhail and her daughter, Eva, lived in a small two-bedroom maisonette, not far from the Thames, the Royal Botanic Gardens, and Kew Palace, an estate used by the British Royal Family from 1728 to 1818. A passionate lover of animals, Olivia had owned dogs her whole life, but when her daughter was four, she noticed another animal was getting all the attention—a pig.

"My daughter watched the movie Babe and absolutely fell in love with it," she remembers. "She watched it every night for weeks and weeks. And then in *Charlotte's Web*, when she put the pig in her pram? Really, she became obsessed with them. Our dogs tragically died sometime later, and it was an awful couple of weeks having no pets in the house. So my daughter started asking for a pig, going on and on, and in the end, I decided: let's look into these pigs."

And so she did her research, for over a year, in fact, much to the impatience of her daughter. It took longer, in part, because Olivia soon saw an opportunity. She discovered an entire world of micro pig breeding, where the animals were clean, cute, and brimming with personality.

The kicker? There was nobody in Greater London breeding or selling these pigs. Olivia was unemployed at the time, so her mind was wide open

Once a tiny operation in a London backyard, Kew Little Pigs has grown to become a major attraction for tourists, school trips, and corporate events. *Credit: Olivia Mikhail.*

to possibilities. But would people actually buy them? Or pay to see them? Her daughter certainly thought so. Then she asked her brother. He said go for it. And that was enough.

So in 2010, with her daughter headed off to school for the first time, Olivia secured a loan and got to work converting her 50-square-foot garden into a miniature pig farm. Her original micro pigs—Kew and Scarlet—took up residence soon thereafter in the backyard. Her first big break came from Moonpig, an online platform where you can create and customize your own greeting cards. The owner of the company loved the idea of spending time with micro pigs so much that he sponsored them to show up at their offices in downtown London once a month.

"Kew became their company pig," Olivia says.

"Kew would play with the staff, and they would take her for walks along the embankment. It allowed me to buy my first van. Then I did all the major pet shows around the country. I did fashion shoots, corporate events. I did my first website. I had some reviews in the local paper. And before I knew it, phones were constantly ringing."

Apparently, micro pigs tucked into a garden on a typical London street was quite the draw. "Pig enthusiasts," as Olivia likes to call them, started to descend on that tiny house in Kew. Siblings would bring their mums; boyfriends brought their girlfriends. People would be in and out all day, especially on the weekends, each handing over a few pounds to frolic or sit with the micro pigs in this curated little farm.

Even Olivia was amazed by the response. Few people wanted to actually buy a micro pig, but they would gladly pay to spend time with them.

"Some people cry. A lot of people get very emotional. They get very excited. A lot of people bring guests without telling them where they are going," she explains. "Mine are very good-looking. They have lovely long eyelashes. If you really know them, and look them in the eye, it is like looking in a human eye. They have characteristics. And they are carefree animals—nothing bothers them."

153

According to Olivia, it rapidly got to the point where the business, while appreciated, became somewhat overwhelming for her modest house.

It was time to expand.

Not long after launching the business, Olivia invested in a field in the countryside to house some of the micro pigs and breed them. By 2014, Kew Little Pigs took on its first farm, and today, according to Olivia, they are the largest micro pig breeder in Europe. Located in Amersham, northwest of London, Kew Little Pigs is an amusement park of micro pig fun, with ten pens spread out over nearly four acres, catering to tourists, school trips, and corporate events from the UK, Europe, and really all over the world.

For her, Eva's fascination for pigs changed her life forever, sparking an entire business—an entire way of life.

Not every story is quite so transformational. I also discovered that sometimes, man and pig can just boil down to a simple friendship.

Ventoi Bethune never cared much for city life, even as a young boy. He had lived in the Bahamian capital of Nassau until he was nine. Then, in 2003, as soon as he was old enough to ride in a boat, off he went to Black Point, the island his family was from.

It was a far cry from Nassau—this community of a few hundred people, just around the corner from Staniel Cay and the swimming pigs, didn't have a store at the corner of each street. It didn't have a corner store at all.

The island worked on generators, which was a luxury, Bethune's granddaddy used to say, compared to when he lived in darkness as a boy. It was the kind of upbringing Munroe, Nicholson's business partner, could relate to on Little Farmer's Cay.

Even in the twenty-first century, Bethune remembers his granddaddy refused to throw out anything, whether it was a piece of rope or a morsel of food.

"He believed it could be used for something else," he explains.

"If there was leftover food on the stove, and it's cold and nobody ate, that food stayed on the stove until it was all gone."

Life revolved around the gathering of food.

Back in the day, the mailboat brought supplies once every two weeks, not like today, when it comes twice a week to these island communities. So Bethune would wake up early in the morning and start fishing with his family. All day, every day, he fished and fished on a tiny boat until dark. Nighttime was spent crabbing, or chasing around land crabs, a popular Bahamian meal.

Bethune would scramble around the island, in the relative pitch-black, the blazing stars above offering some light.

But watch your step—there was no hospital on the island, at least not how most would define it. The nurse was the doctor, the paramedic, and probably the island's teacher, as well. When you live on an island in the Exumas, everyone has multiple jobs. At least Black Point had an airstrip during Bethune's time, if you needed to get out fast. Back in the day, granddaddy said, you'd have to scull in a small boat over to Staniel Cay to get airlifted to Nassau. Nevertheless, Bethune and his family were always acutely aware of the risks.

"Growing up, if you get airlifted to Nassau it had to be serious. Minor stuff you just had to deal with. The nurse would do her best to see how she could remedy," he recalls.

Life didn't change much on the island. When he arrived, he remembers they were building the only bar and restaurant on the island, called Loraine's.

"And they are still building it today," he says with a laugh.

And then there were the swimming pigs, just in Bethune's backyard, really. The pigs were wild back then, he remembers, and not used to human interaction. People visited them occasionally, but nothing like today, not as a full-fledged tourist attraction.

Ventoi Bethune, an inspector at the Bahamas Humane Society, rescued Trevor the Pig in December 2015. They have remained close friends ever since. *Credit: Ventoi Bethune.*

"They were just some pigs on an island that swam for their food," he says.

Bethune always loved animals, which was one reason he joined the Bahamas Humane Society in Nassau many years later, after returning to the capital. Little did he know that pigs would still be very much in his future. In December 2015, Bethune was driving along in the humane society ambulance when we saw a lone pig walking along the side of the road. He screeched to a halt, and as he approached the piglet, only about a month or two old, he made a gruesome discovery—there was a large gash, a bleeding, open wound, down the animal's back. Bethune didn't hesitate; he gently placed the eighteen-pound piglet in the back of the ambulance and, that very afternoon, rushed him into surgery.

"I don't know if he was attacked or what. I think he might have escaped a farm, maybe crawled under a fence and got injured that way," he says.

After the surgery, the piglet got his name—Trevor.

Trevor grew into a celebrity of sorts at the Bahamas Humane Society, even without the status updates, the YouTube videos, the social media accounts, and the Twitter followings. Bethune would take him for walks each day; workers and volunteers from the humane society spoiled him with leftovers from their homes. Trevor, the only pig onsite, quietly developed a kinship with the other animals at the shelter, particularly the

While Trevor is not known as a swimming pig, his favorite pastime is to visit the beach with puppies from his home at the Bahamas Humane Society in Nassau. *Credit: Ventoi Bethune.*

puppies. His favorite thing to do? Hit the beach in Nassau with the dogs. But funny enough, Trevor never turned into a swimming pig. He was just Trevor, Bethune's friend.

"His personality always stood out," Bethune says.

"You can understand what he's saying. The first time we took him to Exuma, it was very hectic for him, and it was the first time he had to be in a cage like that. When we got there, my cousin helped me get him out the cage, and he said: 'Boy . . . this pig is talkin'. He understand!' I swear, if he could say something, if he had the words, he would say it. My plan at first was to take him to the beach with the swimming pigs, but I couldn't leave him. I just want to carry on the relationship. I couldn't leave him."

It might have been the smartest decision he ever made—at least for Trevor's sake.

From South Africa to Canada, to the UK and the Bahamas, the relationship between man and pig is nothing new.

The swimming pigs simply took it up a notch: they popularized it.

Humans are capable of the most remarkable friendships with animals. Conversely, it is no secret that we are also capable of untold destruction. Humanity has always had a rather rocky relationship with the animal kingdom. The swimming pigs would be no different.

CHAPTER 5
Tragedy Strikes

It was a typical Friday afternoon, seemingly like any other. A blizzard was sweeping through Ottawa, and at 3:16 p.m. on February 17, 2017, I was already dreading the inevitable slog home through the frozen tundra, drearily on display out my office window.

Pig Beach seemed a long way away.

At least it's the weekend, I thought. All the things I wanted to do in the coming days were sloshing around in my head as I wrapped up the workweek.

Beep. An email popped up in my inbox.

"Hey—are you in Exuma?"

It was from a tour operator in the Bahamas. The brevity of it all struck me as odd; I had a sense that something was amiss, so I responded immediately.

"No, I'm back in the Ottawa office. What's up?" I replied.

Five long minutes later, he told me.

"Sorry to be brief—many pigs found dead on Big Major's," he wrote. "We are looking into it as much as possible and sending Department of Agriculture down Sunday. Unfortunately don't have much more than that. Will keep you updated."

I hung there in disbelief, staring at the naked words on my screen. I suddenly thought about all the people I could call for information, people who could help. A bit shaky, my fingers hovered over the keyboard: I typed a very simple, but important, question.

"How many dead?" Send.

Two minutes passed. *Beep.* Another email.

"My crew saw 5–6 but only 7 on the beach out of a normal 20. Still a lot unknown right now," the tour operator said.

I asked many other questions, but my source went dark. No doubt he was still gathering information, as well. And I was in Ottawa, helpless. Nothing I could do—I felt a world apart. So I did the only thing I could think of. I worked the phones. I called people to get more details. But to my surprise, most people were equally surprised. For the majority, my call was the first they'd even heard of it.

Swimming pigs dead? How many? How did they die?

All I got were questions, and I had no answers.

That weekend I heard rumors, whispers here and there, but nothing substantiated. I was told that a veterinarian arrived, first on the scene. The humane society and government representatives were flying in from Nassau. Chatter started to spread on social media that the pigs were dead. How could this happen? Who was responsible? What was going on over there? Nobody seemed to know for sure.

The story finally broke on Monday morning, when both the *Nassau Guardian* and the *Tribune* first reported on the incident.

Both newspapers confirmed what we all feared: swimming pigs were dead, but details remained sparse.

The *Nassau Guardian,* my old newspaper, ran the headline: "Seven of Exuma's Famous Swimming Pigs Die."

The paper interviewed Wayde Nixon, the Bahamian widely considered to be the "father" of the original pigs on Big Major Cay, if not the most vocal. He confirmed that a veterinarian and other officials had been treating the colony over the weekend. He called for calm: Pig Beach was still open, and the remaining animals were healthy. About fifteen pigs were still alive, he thought. The whole report was vague. Although the *Nassau Guardian* ran a headline with an exact death count, there was no official number or statement in the story itself. How do they know it was seven? Nobody seemed terribly sure.

And then Nixon said something that would catch the world's attention.

"Right now it's blowing out of proportion with people, anybody bringing food here, anybody doing what they [want to] do," he told the *Nassau Guardian*. "We have people coming there giving the pigs beer, rum, riding on top of them, all kinds of stuff."

Beer, rum, and all kinds of stuff. Oh dear.

A reporter for the *Tribune* interviewed the president of the Bahamas Humane Society, Kim Aranha. Like in the *Guardian*, the cause of death was unclear, but Aranha's initial statement struck a similar cord.

"It could just be a horrible accident where they ate something poisonous," she said.

"It could be malicious, but I don't really see why someone would go out of their way to hurt those lovely animals. I know there are a lot of silly sailors that go and feed them alcohol to try and get them drunk."

Silly sailors trying to get swimming pigs drunk in the Bahamas. Double oh dear.

In today's instant sound-bite world, this was online gold.

The story was a slow burn, but, boy, once it got going, it was a total firestorm.

Among the first to pick it up were *Travel + Leisure* and the Caribbean News Service. The next day, these publications played it more or less straight, regurgitating the information spoon-fed to them by the *Guardian* and *Tribune*. This approach would soon become the standard for hundreds of publications worldwide. There would be no further investigation by these newspapers into what killed the swimming pigs.

It was all based on the same speculative stories. But soon, astoundingly, the story would take a dramatic, sensational turn.

"The famous pigs from *The Bachelor* island date are dying," read a headline on February 23.

161

That's right. there is an "epidemic" on the island, the story declared in the first sentence. Didn't you hear? Only a handful is left, and fading fast. The story went on to refer to a "more sinister twist," citing the swimming pigs possibly being poisoned by alcohol, such as beer and rum. At that point, there was no turning back.

Nixon and Aranha did nothing wrong, mind you; in fact, they expressed very real concerns about how tourists were treating the pigs. They had no idea that these words would be blown up on the world stage.

From here, the incident went viral—from across North America, leaping the pond to Europe, to even as far away as the Far East.

Headline on February 26: "Mystery as Bahamas' Famous Swimming Pigs Are Found Dead—And Local Officials Believe It's because Tourists Are Getting Them Drunk," a British tabloid claimed.

Amy Schumer was among those "last seen" vacationing at Pig Beach, as if we were now reading the world's most bizarre crime novel.

The story was splashed with photos of celebrities in bikinis swimming with the pigs. Teen sensation Bella Thorne, a known animal lover, merited several photos of her feeding the animals. There was even a shot of Donald Trump Jr. and his family making landfall on Big Major Cay, his wife and all five children posing for the camera while a pig buried its face in a bucket of food. In another photo, Vanessa Trump was striking a pose at the front of the boat as if she were surfing.

That article alone had 26,000 shares.

Headline on February 27: "Bahamas' Swimming Pigs Found Dead 'after Tourists Give Them Rum.'"

Why would "after tourists gave them rum" be placed in quotation marks? In the headline, no less? Did anyone actually say those words? Who cares? It got 63,000 shares.

And it just kept spinning: hundreds of articles popped up worldwide, most of them taking on the same theme and appearing in the strangest places. I recall listening to a morning show on an Irish radio station, with Nixon phoning in as the guest.

"They bask in the sun, they swim in the sea. And now seven pigs have been found dead. And they suspect one of the causes of death is tourists giving them rum," the host announced as an introduction to his listeners.

Nixon said: "We know for sure, we watch people and tell them to stop giving them beer and rum. You can't do that, especially the tour boats when people are coming and having a good time. People need to give them water, not rum."

"And has anything like this happened before?" the Irish DJ asked.

"No, we've had the pigs for twenty-seven years and never had a problem," Nixon replied.

The whole interview struck me as a bit tongue in cheek, an odd, perhaps welcome, divergence from world affairs. The Irish DJ concluded by saying: "We have announced we will give up mentioning Donald Trump for Lent. Not mentioning Donald Trump for the next forty days will improve the mental health of the nation to no end."

But it wasn't just dry Irish radio having a bit of fun. The thousands of comments on articles about the dead swimming pigs were often a reflection of the times.

"It was Russian hacking," someone posted.

"All those Commonwealth nations that will flood into Brexit Britain are going to have a wild time feeding local pigs beer & rum and rampaging. Good luck on that one," another said.

"C'mon, we all know what happened. They died from Global Warming," a person commented.

"Perhaps they caught Trump Flu," a reader suggested.

Other comments were completely insensitive to the death of the pigs.

"Well, if the pigs WERE given beer & rum, I would immediately roast them . . . they've already been marinated and should taste pretty good!" someone said.

"Mmmmmmm . . . salted pork!" a reader posted.

It was all so bizarre. The story took on a life of its own. I hate to use the terms "fake news" or "alternative facts," but what else do you call it? The death of the swimming pigs rapidly grew into a media circus, an elaborate, sensational game of broken telephone, where news outlets and their customers believed whatever they wanted to believe. What was true became secondary to entertainment value.

There was no reporting, no due diligence. The same primary sources were used by media outlets around the world, yet the tale changed with each passing day. It morphed into a one-liner, a joke, a punch line, the flavor of the week.

It made me think: What did the deaths of swimming pigs say about us? About how we disseminate and distribute information on the Internet?

What did it say about our empathy toward these animals? Did we truly care? Or did we just want to be entertained? To have something to share? To post? To tweet?

And in all fairness, there were warning signs that something like this could happen to the swimming pigs.

But to be clear—there is no doubt in my mind that no one person is to blame. No Bahamian would ever want such a thing to occur; many of them, especially the tour operators, pour their time and money into looking after the animals. I should also point out that not all pig colonies should be painted with the same brush; Piggyville in Abaco and that second colony located near Grand Isle had no such problems. Overall, the pigs are valued in the Bahamas, both as creatures and for the exposure they bring to the area—the contribution to the economy. And it is easy for outsiders to forget that the Bahamas is not the United States, Canada, or Europe. The Exuma cays are isolated. The means and resources of those who live there are often limited. And sometimes, change can be slow.

You can't view the Bahamas with the same lens.

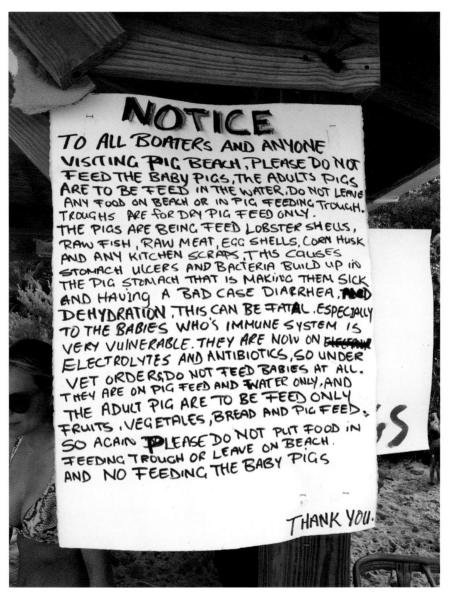

As the swimming pigs surged in popularity, residents of Staniel Cay worked to create rules and regulations to keep the attraction safe. *Credit: T. R. Todd.*

Not to mention people don't appreciate just how fast the attraction exploded. I think it caught some by surprise.

I have visited the swimming pigs dozens of times; not once have I been bitten by a pig. And yet, we started to hear cases of the occasional nip. Nobody was seriously hurt, to my knowledge, but it was concerning nonetheless. In my opinion, the issue had more to do with the dramatic rise in tourists, as opposed to the behavior of the animals; the swimming pigs were not to blame. What happens when you have a few hundred people visiting these animals for twenty-five years or so, and suddenly, in the span of two years, or less, you have thousands? How many times have you heard a sad story of human encroachment and its impact on an animal's habitat and behavior?

Tourists also forget these are indeed wild animals.

With thousands of additional people going there, inevitably, you will have guests not quite sure how to interact with the pigs properly.

"They are friendly, but you have to be careful. People get their fingers bit, or got their bottoms bit. So you have to be careful and respect them," said Russell, the Pig Whisperer of Abaco.

"They call me the Pig Whisperer and I still don't feed them by hand."

It was also only a matter of time before other animal lovers had their say. The vegan community would soon get involved, pointing out that the conditions under which the swimming pigs lived could be much better. The swimming pigs could use more shelter and have an improved diet of fruits and vegetables.

Speaking of diet: another issue, because of the sheer volume of people, was overfeeding. Many tour operators looked after the swimming pigs admirably, bringing them food and water daily. Of course, the tourists wanted to feed them, too, because that was what made them swim, right? So what happens when they're too well fed? They stop swimming, on occasion. Apparently, even a pig can have enough.

Many of the swimming pigs have grown to become quite large over the years. Local experts advise tourists to avoid feeding the animals by hand. *Credit: Amanda Parlee.*

These were some of the early signs that the attraction was due for a correction.

More than a week had passed since the local press had first reported the deaths. The story had gone around the globe, and it didn't appear to be slowing down anytime soon. That changed, however, on March 1, when the ruling government at the time, the Progressive Liberal Party (PLP), issued a statement.

"The report is in place, I have not had the chance to digest the total contents of it, but I am satisfied that the pigs died from ingestion of sand material," a cabinet minister said.

"As you know, some people feed the pigs as they swim in the water, other people throw things on the sand for them to eat from the sand. You know sand is indigestible, sand cannot be digested, and the autopsy which was performed on one or two of the animals showed that they had a good amount of sand in their stomach. Sand not being able to be passed out by normal processes or digested had something to do with those animals having died. They died because of that kind of ingestion. That's the conclusion the veterinarian drew from his autopsy. We've sent blood samples off to labs to be tested to see whether there is any other contributing factor but to him that was the main cause, preliminarily found to have affected the lives of those animals."

The findings were met with intense skepticism.

Hadn't the pigs lived on the beach for nearly three decades? Why now? Why would they suddenly die from eating too much sand when they had lived there for so long? And why would so many die all at once?

Is it possible they were poisoned?

The international press picked up on the autopsy report immediately, serving up a fresh angle and headline for the story.

To add further confusion to the mix, the *Tribune* released a story the next day revealing that farmers were at a "breaking point" over widespread contaminated feed in Nassau. According to the report, large amounts of corn had been improperly stored and turned rancid, and many animals, including pigs, were dying.

Did any of that feed make it to the tour operators and into the mouths of the pigs?

The mystery deepened. Nobody seemed to know the truth; there were so many stories and rumors. Funny enough, there has always been something about the swimming pigs that sparks the imagination. It reminded me of when we shot the film and explored all those theories of how the pigs got there in the first place.

The swimming pigs were just as mysterious in life as they were in death.

I decided right then and there: it was time to do a little digging of my own.

For years, Amanda Parlee had traveled from Canada to Staniel Cay to see the pigs swim. It was a special spot for Amanda and her husband. It all started when their eldest daughter showed them a video of the pigs online a few years back, and they immediately made the bucket list. Amanda went for the pigs but got hooked on the beauty and people of Exuma.

"We've fallen in love with the Bahamas," she says. "So we just keep going there now, to Exuma. It is such a gem there. We love it."

It was their third year in a row visiting Staniel Cay and Pig Beach, back in February 2017. By now, she had a pretty good idea what to expect. They landed at Staniel Cay Airport and were greeted by that incredible blue water, plenty of familiar faces, and friendly staff. The quaint oceanside cottages came with a rental boat, allowing them to visit Pig Beach, Thunderball Grotto, or any of the local islands and attractions at their leisure. The week started off as it always had, another trip in paradise, in the truest sense of the word. A few days later, Amanda and her husband met and befriended a newcomer to the island, Carolina Fernandez, a veterinarian all the way from Argentina, traveling with her boyfriend, who had made the trip specifically to see the swimming pigs.

"I met Carolina the day prior to her going to the island at the Staniel Cay Yacht Club. I had been there [Pig Beach] that day but did not notice any of the pigs being sick," Parlee recalls. "She was so excited to be going the following day."

Carolina was no ordinary veterinarian—"the queen of pigs" might be a more fitting description. With a home in Buenos Aires, she rises at 6 a.m. every Monday to drive twenty miles to a small town called San Antonio de Areco. There you will find a pig farm with, according to Carolina, no fewer than eight thousands pigs.

Carolina doesn't eat pork. And she loves pigs. Although the farm is industrial, raising and butchering the pigs for food, Carolina is passionate about ensuring these animals have a decent quality of life.

For up to ten hours a day, the official veterinarian of this industrial pig farm treats and cares for the pigs. The job is so consuming that she doesn't leave San Antonio de Areco all week; she stays in her apartment there until Friday and then spends the weekend back in the capital.

"I know they are finally going to the supermarket, but I want them to have a better life while they are at the farm," Carolina explains.

"I encourage people to treat them well. You don't have to hit them and you can provide good conditions for them. I think pigs are very smart. If you teach them something, they will learn. You have to be patient. For example, sometimes when they are in one place, and I need them to go to another place, I do it quietly. I always speak with them. They know me, so they just do it."

Carolina said that she always has a special place for sick pigs at the farm, and many of them recover.

"I don't want anyone to kill the ones that are sick. I treat them," she says.

With such a passion for pigs, one can imagine her excitement at the prospect of hanging out with swimming pigs in one of the most beautiful places on Earth.

However, as if by providence, Carolina was about to step into a desperate situation.

On the morning of February 16, as planned, she rented a boat to go swim with the pigs—the purpose for her traveling more than four thousand miles. Carolina was positively bubbly after her conversation with Amanda the previous night; she had no reason to suspect anything was wrong. But from the moment she arrived, Carolina had a sinking feeling in her gut. Something wasn't right.

"When I walked around the island, I saw there was a little piglet that was lying down beside a tree," Carolina remembers.

"I went there and he was really sick. I told the man who I rented the boat from—'He needs medicine.' The man was very upset about it. 'Okay,' he said. 'Let's go get some medicine for this pig.'"

Everyone was concerned, according to Carolina, even the shopkeeper when they arrived at the tiny pharmacy on Staniel Cay. Carolina's first diagnosis was clear—the piglet was badly dehydrated, he needed fluids, so she bought a saline solution to inject into the animal. With her own money, Carolina swiftly purchased the needles, materials, and medications. She knew time was not her friend. Then the boat captain zipped her back to Pig Beach to find the sick piglet.

It was around this time that, according to Carolina, she found the first dead pig. But she didn't have time to think. First, she administered fluids to the piglet, struggling to find a vein.

"After that, I waited for the piglet to get better. He woke up eventually and seemed to be better. He could move around and drink water. I was feeling good about that," she recalls.

Shocked and confused, but feeling a high from her small victory, Carolina decided to take a break and go for lunch. But it was a troubled meal; it didn't feel like a holiday anymore. It wasn't long before she felt compelled to return and check up on her patient. Unfortunately, according to Carolina, what she found was far worse than she expected—more dead

Carolina Fernandez, a veterinarian from Argentina, treated many of the ailing and dying pigs on Pig Beach. She believes dehydration played a key role in their decline. *Credit: Amanda Parlee.*

bodies on Pig Beach. By now, word had spread that the swimming pigs were in trouble. Carolina met Nixon and a few other Bahamians for the first time; everyone was trying to get a handle on the situation. Nixon had popped an achilles tendon, making it difficult for him to trudge around the beach in a supportive boot. Don Rolle was off island. It was a confusing time; nobody was quite sure what to do next.

When Nixon found out Carolina was a veterinarian, he asked her for help. She offered to perform an autopsy, of sorts.

"So we put three pigs into a boat," according to Carolina. "Two little ones and one very big. I went into the boat with him, and we went into the middle of the ocean so nobody can see us opening the pigs. I opened the pigs and saw what was wrong with them."

She found sand in their bowels and stomach, verifying the findings that would be released later by the government.

However, that wasn't what ultimately killed them, according to Carolina. Some of the pigs had ulcers on their stomachs, she reported, implying there was an issue with their diet. One of the pigs had a plastic bag inside. Overall, she found their insides to be "very, very dry," including the undigested food in their stomachs.

"They were very dehydrated. They have to take all the water out of the food. I found them to be very white and anemic," she reported.

By this time, Amanda and her husband had heard about the medical emergency on Pig Beach, and how their friend from Argentina was at the very center of it. They lent whatever help they could as the veterinarian went to work. Amanda brought water and fruit from Staniel Cay to feed the pigs. Carolina returned to the pharmacy and purchased more medication. It was at this time that the pharmacist put her on the phone with a veterinarian from Nassau, who worked for the government, to explain the situation.

Time is of the essence, she said. These are the medicines I need. This is what must be done.

173

Don't worry, the person on the phone said. A plane will be arriving tomorrow morning at 8:30 a.m. with all the medicine you'll need.

At that time, on Friday, February 17, she looked to Staniel Cay's skies with anticipation: but no plane came.

She didn't have time to fret. One of the guests at Staniel Cay, a regular from Tennessee, told her to come quick; there were more sick pigs on the beach. So the two of them went back to the pharmacy, loaded up with medicine, and roared back to Pig Beach. Some of the larger pigs were difficult to treat—they didn't understand that their lives were in danger.

"I tried to catch a big one with a rope, but he was very aggressive," she remembers. "It was difficult. I did catch him in the end and injected him with some medicine. I only managed to give him a small dose of the medicine, though. I don't know what happened to that pig in particular."

Friday was spent mostly this way: chasing down pigs, treating them, seeing many of them recover. But several pigs died that day too, according to Carolina, and were given a burial at sea. She also spoke on the phone once again with the veterinarian from Nassau. We are coming, she was assured. And indeed, the next afternoon, the veterinarian arrived.

Local police had closed the beach to tourists as officials tried to get a handle on the crisis. Carolina told them everything she could. Although the situation seemed more or less stable on the beach, when pigs don't feel well, they tend to withdraw and hide. Big Major Cay is not a small island, after all. So Carolina, the veterinarian from Nassau, and a few others ventured into the bush in search of more patients.

It was then that they made a grim discovery.

"We went to find the fountain of freshwater, and there wasn't really any at all. It had all dried up. It was dirty," according to Carolina.

In fact, according to multiple sources, Exuma had been going through a drought in the lead-up to the tragedy. This assessment was later confirmed by the Caribbean Drought and Precipitation Monitoring Network, which reported that the Bahamas had experienced an unusually dry January and advised several Caribbean nations to monitor the situation closely.

The unusual scarcity of water was also reported in an article by *National Geographic*, titled "This Is What Really Killed the Famous Swimming Pigs."

Remember Bethune, owner of Trevor the Pig?

He arrived in Pig Beach on the Saturday, along with rest of the cavalry, to represent the Bahamas Humane Society. He later confirmed to *National Geographic* that most of the freshwater on the island had dried up. He also offered perhaps the most evenhanded and reasonable explanation so far: it probably wasn't just one thing that killed the swimming pigs, but rather a combination of factors over a period of time.

With a record number of tourists, severe drought, and visitors feeding them things they shouldn't, even the mighty pig may have reached a tipping point. To add insult to injury, probably the most common food given to the pigs, bread, was often fed to them while they were swimming, marinated in salt water. Not the tastiest treat for an animal already dehydrated.

"There are things being printed internationally that I don't think are correct," a board member of the Bahamas Humane Society later told me.

"Their water supply was almost completely dried up. Without enough freshwater, any kind of foreign substance in their system that their body couldn't handle got that much worse. Some of them just became very weak and died. Pigs should be able to handle just about anything, but not having enough water could really upset their immune system. We've had huge arguments with people right there on the beach, regarding [feeding them] liquor."

She wasn't the only one. Amanda said that, while Carolina was treating the pigs, she confronted a boatload of people down the beach. As Carolina administered lifesaving treatment, Amanda spotted someone pouring a beer down a pig's throat.

Carolina Fernandez takes a moment to enjoy the swimming pigs of Exuma. Despite the unexpected difficulties during her visit, Carolina said she would love to visit Pig Beach again. *Credit: Amanda Parlee.*

"I pretty much went nuclear like some crazy woman," Amanda recalls. "I went over there and said to them: 'What do you think you're doing?! This isn't even funny!'"

In a way, the health of the swimming pigs is all of our responsibility.

As for Carolina, she worked all of Saturday to stabilize the rest of the colony. The next morning, as she waited for her plane, someone told her that that they had left food and medicine overnight on the beach for the pigs they couldn't catch and give injections to. They went to see if the food was still there in the morning, and it was gone.

That made Carolina feel better as she boarded her flight home, more than four thousand miles back to Argentina. In a few days, she would return to work at the pig farm, offering treatment and comfort to animals bound for the slaughterhouse.

What a coincidence. What a strange circumstance—some might call fate—that Carolina would be in Exuma when the pigs needed her most.

"It was a godsend that she was there. It could have been a lot worse," Amanda says.

For Nixon, he never fully accepted Carolina's findings. In fact, he maintains to this day that the swimming pigs were deliberately poisoned.

"Somebody poisoned them. That's what I think," he says. "After all of that, we are still trying to figure out who poisoned the pigs. We have been here for years and never had that problem before."

So did the swimming pigs die from drinking too much rum? Was it poor diet and dehydration? Or perhaps it was a combination of factors? Was it the spoiled and contaminated feed from Nassau? Is it possible there was foul play at work? Someone with an axe to grind? Could the pigs have been intentionally poisoned?

In short, how do we solve this mystery of the dead pigs?

We may never know for sure. Whatever the explanation might be, the reason for their deaths should be secondary to where we go from here.

Bernadette Chamberlain, who owns a restaurant on Staniel Cay, helped establish a nursery for the piglets to ensure their good health. Chamberlain is one of many locals who have stepped up to help make the swimming pigs a sustainable attraction. *Credit: T. R. Todd.*

In the days that followed, changes were made on the beach. Signs were put up discouraging people from feeding the pigs destructive substances, or riding them and engaging in inappropriate behavior. A trough was installed, creating a designated place to feed them so that they don't ingest an excess of sand or salt water. An enclosure was built for shelter.

Discussions began about creating a roped-off area for the pigs to swim in at particular hours of the day. Locals could sell "pig-approved" food to the tourists when they arrived, rather than allowing people to feed them whatever they wanted.

Sometimes, bad things must happen to make way for the good—a jolt of reality.

After all, the attraction happened by accident. More than twenty-five years of anonymity to a few years of stardom: we saw the impact of that.

Remarkably, the community responded. Bernadette Chamberlain, that lady who owns a restaurant on Staniel Cay, stepped up with her husband and raised enough money to buy proper water tanks for the island. If dehydration was a reason for the deaths, having a consistent source of water would make a huge difference. She now takes water out to the tanks every three or four days, and they even built a guttering system to ensure the pigs receive water, even when they aren't around. Just down from the enclosure, they built a nursery for the piglets to ensure they receive proper care and nutrition after birth.

Ever since the tragedy, Chamberlain, among others, has found herself to be a constant custodian of the swimming pigs.

"A couple days ago some of them were sick," she says.

"So I called the veterinarian in Nassau, and we've been sure to give them enough electrolytes. We put vitamins in their water. Recently, one of them got cut, I so I had to go the nurse and get some things, to bandage him, after he got cut by a boat's propeller. It is a community effort. These pigs are definitely part of our history now. We name the pigs after legends from the island. Rolle Gray—he was a legend from sailing. Al was the reverend. Hugh was the deacon. And Momma Blanche, she was the mom for the whole island, and then Hansel, who was one of the main pig farmers back from the old days. We name them from the older generations of the islands."

From pork to pampered legends, the evolution was amazing to see. And it wasn't just the island of Staniel Cay that rallied around the swimming pigs.

The story of the pigs' deaths continued to echo online for weeks, in publications around the world. There were many reasons for that, I came to appreciate.

Yes, the story went viral because of our appetite for the shocking, unusual, and sensational, our lust for social media and sharing.

I think some of the reactions were disingenuous, without any sincere concern for the animals.

But the further I looked into it, the less cynical I became. I realized that there were people who really cared about their welfare. People were upset. Outraged.

Although this tragedy was a far more serious case, it reminded me of Hurricane Matthew, when there was a genuine outpouring of concern, even grief, for the pigs' well-being during the storm.

Years later, Hurricane Dorian would stir up these feelings all over again.

This hurricane, a category 5 storm, walloped the northern Bahamas in August 2019 with sustained winds of 185 miles per hour. For Grand Bahama and Abaco, it left complete devastation in its wake, with seventy-four people reported dead, and hundreds more missing. Not long after landfall, concerns began to circulate online, prompting Ray and Justin Lightbourn, owners of the tour boat company Exuma Water Sports and curators of The Swimming Pigs Instagram account, to issue a statement:

Notice to all concerned about the welfare of The Swimming Pigs: Hurricane Dorian did NOT affect The Swimming Pigs in Exuma, they are fine, but it has basically destroyed the Northern Bahamas. We have been receiving numerous emails and messages from around the world and cannot possibly answer them all. Thank you though for all of the kind thoughts. The people and pets of Abaco will need help for sure though.

So then the question became—what about the pigs in Abaco? Considering the images coming out of these islands, the situation looked grim. The islands had been decimated by goliath-sized storm surges, in some cases more than twenty feet high. There were biting winds that tore every leaf off every tree.

Social media was abuzz with this question—did they survive?

The answer came several days later—yes, miraculously, the pigs on No Name Cay were alive. Ryan Schiedel, a charter boat captain from Port Canaveral, Florida, posted a video of the pigs being given food and water, surrounded by skeletal trees.

I had to find out what happened for myself.

"We knew the Bahamas was going to get hit badly, so I decided that I wanted to run supplies down there to help people out," Schiedel told me.

For Schiedel, Abaco was a second home. As a child, he would take fishing trips to the island with his family. This tradition would later become his livelihood. Many of the people in Abaco were his best friends. So this relief mission was more than a good deed—it was personal. Schiedel and a few friends packed his boat with just about everything you can imagine—bathroom supplies, canned food, tents, and water.

"We went over there and saw it and looked around. It looked like a nuclear bomb hit the place. It was crazy. I've never seen anything close," he remembers.

First, Schiedel and his crew went to Green Turtle Cay, a popular tourism community. Everyone formed a procession line and helped unload and distribute supplies. He remembers seeing so many relief boats that day. In fact, there were so many boats, he still had some extra supplies and fresh water.

No Name Cay was nearby. Schiedel and his friends looked at each other and thought—let's go check on the swimming pigs.

But they found more than they bargained for.

"The only structure on the island was a new restaurant and bar they had built," he recalls. "And it was not standing; it was all knocked down. But they had some sort of shelter as well, and that's where they stayed with the pigs."

Wait? Who were they?

"There were a couple Haitian men, the island caretakers. I don't think anyone knew they were there. They were cut and beat up pretty good," Schiedel says.

Despite the destruction around them, man and pig seemed healthy.

Schiedel and his friends dressed their wounds. They left the rest of their supplies and filled up the pigs' water tanks.

"Those pigs led us to helping human life we didn't know was there," he adds.

"We were able to drop off supplies for those living on the island, riding out the storm and looking after animals. They were there on their own, no way to get off the island. Without the pigs, we never would have known they were there."

I sometimes imagine what it must have been like in that dark shelter, on a small island with no means of escape. I think about those roaring winds and the sounds those men must have heard. And there, right beside them, were the swimming pigs, with an equal opportunity for survival.

They were looking out for those pigs, even under the most terrifying, life-threatening circumstances.

And when Schiedel announced the pigs were alive, social media rejoiced. People were thrilled by the news. In that moment, all lives were equal.

So it's clear—people do care about these animals. And like so many other people, when those swimming pigs died on Big Major Cay in Exuma, I was upset. I wanted to know why it happened. I also felt a sense of outrage and concern. I needed answers.

As a society, we are capable of such compassion. We can have an outpouring of concern for these animals, but it often doesn't match our day-to-day actions.

How many millions of pigs are farmed and killed inhumanely by industrial farming? How many more end up, one way or another, in retail products we buy every day?

I was just like Fern: I wanted to save Wilbur, but my kitchen smelled like bacon.

Why so much outrage over a few dead pigs on a secluded island?

To find some answers, and benefit from a different point of view, I asked Hal Herzog, a professor of psychology at Western Carolina University. Herzog has studied animal activists, animal researchers, and circus animal trainers, all in an effort to better understand our real-world ethical dilemmas as they relate to animals.

In his book *Some We Love, Some We Hate, Some We Eat: Why It's So Hard to Think Straight about Animals,* he considers these moral conundrums, many of which offer fascinating insight into our society as a whole.

For Herzog, a sense of outrage over the death of the swimming pigs juxtaposed with our overall acceptance of systematic abuse toward animals (notwithstanding the vegan and vegetarian communities) is not altogether surprising. He argues it is yet another example, albeit a very high profile and poignant one, of our "ability to live with inconsistency." In the 1950s, the eminent psychologist Leon Festinger coined the term "cognitive dissonance," or the theory that we cannot hold two contradictory ideas at the same time. In other words, if we have a particular belief, idea, or value, but we perform actions or thoughts that contradict it, we will ultimately become motivated to change something in the way we think or act to make peace with ourselves, even though the contradiction still exists. Put simply, we lie to ourselves to create a sense of comfort.

"That is really the human condition, and we see it all over the place," Herzog explains.

"Pigs are interesting for many reasons. And the thing they have going against them is they taste really good. That is the problem."

It is also a problem, apparently, for self-proclaimed vegetarians, if you believe the research. According to recent studies, including one conducted by the U.S. Department of Agriculture in 2013, around 13,000 Americans were randomly interviewed over the phone about their eating habits. Only 3 percent of those surveyed identified as not eating meat. According to the study, when these individuals were surveyed again a week later, 66 percent admitted to having eaten meat in recent days.

Were people lying? Do they have different definitions of what constitutes vegetarianism? Or is it possible that we have a particularly complex relationship with animals?

"If you ask Americans, or Canadians, we are generally a nation of animal lovers," Herzog says.

"By my calculations, we spend something in the realm of $5 billion a year in animal protection but fifty times that on killing animals, if you include recreational hunting, animal research, and, in particular, the animals we eat."

He offered another example: the case of Pale Male the hawk, a notorious resident high atop a luxury apartment building on Fifth Avenue in Manhattan, who had a nest there since 1990. In 2004, antipigeon spikes, which had long anchored the nest, were removed by the building's board; apparently, according to the *New York Times*, the hawks were creating an awful mess down below.

The removal of the nest sparked an international outcry; there were protests, environmental organizations got involved, and there was even intervention by some of the area's celebrity residents. Eventually, under tremendous pressure, the nest and Pale Male returned to the original site.

Are the famous swimming pigs of Exuma another case of an overblown crusade? Do we lose the plot with these flash points? The big picture?

The point, according to Herzog, is not to disparage those who make a genuine commitment to veganism, vegetarianism, or animal rights. Instead, moments like these allow us, as a wider society, to take a closer look at what we truly believe. It sheds light on a very real schizophrenic relationship with the animal kingdom.

When it comes to Exuma, I have no doubt the people there love the swimming pigs. They have brought prosperity to many who truly needed it. And it has given thousands upon thousands of people from all around the world a new appreciation for the pig; they get to interact with the animal in a completely new and original way. After the pigs died, change was required, but there have been a lot of positives, too.

"It hasn't stopped us from going," Amanda says, "but it makes me want to spread awareness. Because the people there are beautiful. You are part of the family. If there is something we can all do together, I am all for it. We just want to help."

Carolina couldn't hide her disappointment, but at the same time, she also looked to the future with hope.

"I was happy in one part, because I got to help the pigs," she says.

"I thought I was going to have a relaxing holiday in my place in the world. Pigs in paradise is everything for me. I was disappointed, but all the people on Staniel Cay were worried about the pigs. They loved them. I think some changes will be made now. I do want to go back."

CHAPTER 6
Wish for Coexistence

J illian Crockett and the swimming pigs share one thing in common—
they don't sweat.

But this beautiful seven-year-old girl from Westchester, Maryland,
doesn't let her condition slow her down. Bubbly and active, Jillian loves
nothing more than to play outside, jump in the water, and, as her mother
describes it, "stay active from sunup to sundown." You would never know
that beneath her shirt is a hybrid cooling vest, a state-of-the-art piece of
equipment that compensates for her inability to cool herself down by
sweating. It doesn't bother Jillian one bit. In fact, she enjoys showing off
her gadget in the playground.

"I don't sweat! That's why I'm wearing this! It keeps me cool!" she
often declares.

Jillian's inability to sweat is just one aspect of her condition, which
Rachel, her mom, said is "complicated." Her daughter lives with what is
considered a rare genetic and metabolic problem that affects her central
nervous system. Although her medical issues are numerous, Rachel said
Jillian's main problem is a form of epilepsy called Doose syndrome, where
the patient endures seizures and loses muscle tone. In other words, the
body, amid the spasms, simply stops working.

"It has resulted, unfortunately, in bloody noses, concussions. We've had
busted mouths. She had one where it killed the tooth because she hit a
metal bar in the playground," Rachel explains.

In April 2017, Jillian Crockett, left, seen here with her brother, Andy, got to visit Pig Beach as part of the Make-A-Wish Foundation. Since the trip, the foundation has reported more wishes to see the Swimming Pigs. *Credit: Rachel Crockett.*

Jillian also has neuropathy, Rachel explains, that affects all of her extremities and gives her burning and pain. She has difficulty balancing and walking at times.

Jillian refuses to let these challenges slow her down. The family's life, however, revolves around her unique needs. With therapies and appointments several times a week, sometimes out of state, Jillian is homeschooled because she isn't able to attend enough classes to pass a grade. Every movement, every life decision, must be carefully considered. She receives some form of treatment every three hours. Rachel had to quit her job in the state's attorney's office to be with her daughter full time. Her husband, Dan, supports the family through his job with the Carroll County government office in Westminster.

Jillian has intolerance to cold as well, making outings in the winter months more difficult. For the summer, her high-tech cooling vest has special lightweight ice packs on the inside that freeze quickly and easily.

"In her case, because she doesn't sweat, the heat collects under her skin, so she gets itchy, and it can cause seizures when she gets really hot," Rachel says. "If we are out somewhere and we can't recharge the packs in time, the vest is made out of a fabric you can soak in water, and that works really well."

Similarly, it is a little-known fact that pigs have such small sweat glands that they basically don't sweat at all, forcing them to take alternative measures, such as rolling around in mud.

It has absolutely nothing to do with wanting to be dirty.

Funny enough, Jillian had no idea they shared this genetic quirk when she watched a YouTube video of the swimming pigs in paradise for the first time. And a second time. Rachel didn't know it then, but her daughter was secretly dreaming about those pigs.

Nobody saw what was coming next.

Unbeknownst to Rachel, Jillian's grandmother had nominated her for the Make-A-Wish Foundation, an organization that aims to grant a wish for every child diagnosed with a life-threatening medical condition. Incredibly, the foundation, with tens of thousands of volunteers and donors, grants a wish for a child in the United States every thirty-four minutes.

After receiving a call telling her Jillian had been chosen, Rachel answered a knock at the door in September 2016 to find volunteers Laura and Jim ready for a friendly chat. Rachel remembers they brought a little bag of toys for both her daughter and son, Andy. Laura and Jim sat Jillian down at the kitchen table and asked her a very simple question—if you could do anything, anything in the world, and not have to worry about money or medical visits, what would you do?

Jillian knew immediately: "I want to swim with the pigs," she said, beaming.

189

Laura and Jim sat there in silence, stunned. Swim with the pigs?

Now that's something you don't hear every day.

Before visiting your home, the foundation provides a pamphlet showing you some examples of a typical wish. Many children want to visit Walt Disney World in Orlando, Florida. Others might want to meet their childhood hero, like a celebrity or professional athlete. Or perhaps the child wants to be an airline pilot, ballerina, or princess for a day. But swimming with pigs on a secluded island in the Bahamas? That was a new one.

"They had no idea what it was," Rachel says, laughing.

"So I had to get the computer and find the video, and show them what she wanted to do. They were extremely excited. Everyone in the organization was excited, because it was a brand-new adventure for them. It was the first time ever that someone wanted to swim with the pigs. At first, I think she wanted to go to Disney and see the princesses. But after that video, all she wanted was to see the swimming pigs. We thought after a while she would change her mind, but she didn't."

It was a tall order for the Make-A-Wish Foundation.

First off, Pig Beach is isolated, with very little access to specialized medical care. And let's not forget—it's a tropical island, and Jillian doesn't sweat. But if the pigs can make it, so could Jillian. Laura and Jim insisted that the foundation would do everything they could to make it happen.

"We had not granted a wish to swim with the pigs before, but actually since Jillian's wish, we have a new request to swim with the pigs in our pipeline now," says Kellie Wyatt, head of marketing for the Make-A-Wish Foundation for the Atlantic region.

"When she came to us with her wish, we had to consult with her doctors and nurses. All of our wishes have to be approved by the child's medical provider before we move forward with them. I had heard of them [the swimming pigs] because I watched them on *The Bachelor*. I think they have gained some notoriety in the media as of late, and on TV, and you see people talking about them on social media. Once the wish came through, we were super excited. We thought it was an amazing idea. I want to swim with the pigs myself."

Two months later, the family got another phone call—get those goggles and swimsuits ready, Jillian is swimming with the pigs!

The trip was planned for the following spring, giving the Make-A-Wish Foundation and the Crocketts plenty of time to consider every detail and contingency.

In addition to working directly with Jillian's doctors, Wyatt said Jillian's family had to be "up for adventure." In other words, this trip was no stroll through Disney World. However, according to Wyatt, that is exactly why she believes swimming with the pigs could be the next big thing for the Make-A-Wish Foundation.

It makes for a new, authentic, once-in-a-lifetime experience.

"We get requests to swim with dolphins, or go to Africa to see some exotic animal, but this could be the next big thing," she says.

"We have sixty-two other chapters through the U.S. and forty international affiliates. We are all independently run, but I have a feeling there are other Make-A-Wish chapters seeing this come across their radars now."

And sure enough, in April 2017, Rachel, Andy, and, of course, Jillian all landed on Staniel Cay to make her wish come true.

"The staff at Staniel Cay were so amazing and wonderful," Rachel remembers. "The first night we were there, they brought out desserts with little paper pigs on them. They were all so overwhelmingly nice and excited to be able to help with her wish. That really made a lasting impression on us. Everyone was beyond hospitable."

The next day, on a private boat, the family set off from Staniel Cay to Pig Beach. Jillian, suited up in her hybrid cooling vest, was a bit nervous at first; she had never been on a boat before, especially a speedboat on the ocean, the waves crashing up and down. But as the vessel slowed down, and the bow lowered to eye level, Jillian spotted something in the distance.

She scrambled to the very front of the boat, pointing and screaming with excitement.

"Look! They're swimming out to the boat! Look at them!" she screamed.

And there they were—the swimming pigs of Exuma.

The adult pigs swimming around the boat were bigger than Jillian had expected, as she threw some food to them from the boat. The piglets were resting on the beach. However, that wouldn't stop this energetic girl who loved to swim.

Determined, Jillian jumped in the water, and according to Rachel, the pigs were very well behaved with their honored guest. Rachel recalls they were so worried about the hot tropical weather in Exuma. Would the cooling vest be enough? As it turned out, the family didn't plan for the ocean being a bit chilly. They soon discovered what keeps the pigs so cool in their private piece of paradise. Jillian stayed in the crisp ocean water for so long—swimming, feeding, and playing with the pigs—that her lips turned blue. It was time to climb back in the boat and watch for a while, bundled up in a towel and in her mother's arms.

Rachel says her daughter still beams back in Westminster when they remember their trip to the Exumas. Jillian talks about going back all the time, Rachel says, laughing, and about how she needs to find a rich boyfriend who will take her there on dates.

Kidding aside, it was the look on her daughter's face, perched at the front of the boat, spotting those pigs swimming in surreal blue water, that made it so special.

"It was a huge help to us, to have the chance to do an amazing trip where they have planned everything and all issues when traveling abroad," Rachel says. "It meant a lot to us. It meant a lot to see Jillian so happy."

Amid the constant barrage of selfies, articles, and videos, I find it can all be a bit of a blur; the swimming pigs, over time, almost seem to become living and breathing props for our social media–obsessed world.

And then, when a handful of the pigs died, it was easy to grow cynical about the relationship between man and beast.

It made me wonder: does humanity always find a way to screw it up?

Then I stumbled across Jillian Crockett's story. After she returned from Exuma, her life didn't get any easier. The family increased her epilepsy medications when the seizures got worse. Rachel and her husband would constantly search for new treatments to help their seven-year-old daughter.

"She is still her happy, smiling self! You'd never know!" Rachel says with a laugh.

A wish to visit the swimming pigs of Exuma was ultimately a brief moment in time. Reality soon returned for the Crocketts of Westminster, Maryland.

But it reminded me, in a very powerful way, that the swimming pigs bring people joy.

Maybe that's the reason, deep down, we can't get enough of them. Whimsical, innocent, and playful, they remind us that it's okay not to take life so seriously. We can let go of whatever challenges, restraints, or problems we have in our lives and just watch pigs swim. Something about the animal, perhaps all that cultural, religious, and sociological baggage, makes them perfect ambassadors for this joy.

In the end, Jillian and the swimming pigs have more in common than a lack of sweat: they inspire us to appreciate life, no matter what, in all its forms.

So if the swimming pigs bring us so much happiness and wonder, if they can be the subject of a little girl's only wish, if they offer a new and unusual way to interact with a pig, then there must be a sustainable way forward on Pig Beach.

All of the changes to the attraction, like the signage, feeding stations, and shelters, are certainly a good start.

Ventoi Bethune supports the marking off of buoys to create designated swimming areas for the pigs, while also keeping tourists out in the water on their boats as much as possible. Only the tour boat operators and Pig Beach caretakers would be allowed on the island for any period of time. This practice, he argues, will ensure the pigs keep swimming out to the boats and eliminate issues of the animals being mistreated. Overall, he says the tour guides do an admirable job educating and monitoring guests they bring, but you can't police everyone all the time. Given the popularity of the attraction, perhaps the time has come for a full-time "park warden," of sorts.

Amanda Parlee agrees that you need someone "policing the island to ensure visitors are actually obeying the signs."

It is a fair point. Tourists also have a responsibility to treat the animals with respect. Chamberlain goes so far as to say that people "need to stop treating the pigs as garbage disposal."

"People feed them everything from raw meat and raw fish, to lobster shells, egg shells, and it messes up their stomachs. We suggest vegetables, fruit, and bread," he says.

The swimming pigs near Staniel Cay also need a more consistent source of freshwater, Parlee adds, to hedge against any future droughts. And thanks to Chamberlain and some others in the community, the original pig beach has that now. This system, along with the giant water tank installed at the new pig colony in Abaco, would make a lot of sense for all of the pig communities.

Craig "Pig Whisperer" Russell takes it a step further.

"We need some kind of association and have a veterinarian cycling through these populations," he says. "But it needs to be something where you collect money to pay for these expenses of the association. It is also probably best to get the males neutered."

The Pig Whisperer is making sense. And in Eleuthera and Spanish Wells, Thomas and Chuck Pinder did exactly that—they charged ten dollarsper person to land on the island, which went towards food, medical bills, and a full-time caretaker. Bruce Pinder, as a tour boat operator, simply passed this cost along to the consumer. Won't most people be willing to pay just a bit extra, if they know the money is helping the animals? The real issue is this—with so many pig colonies showing up in the country, how do you police them all? Right now, not all pig colonies are created equal. In fact, many tourists do not realize there are multiple pig colonies and end up criticizing everyone based on one experience.

Nigel Bowe, from Powerboat Adventures, believes the Bahamas, as an archipelago, would be too difficult to police effectively. Bowe, who has his own island in Ship Channel Cay, has the unique ability to ensure his experience is pristine.

"I think the industry has to self-regulate to keep healthy pigs," he says.

Meanwhile, Barbara Darville, in Grand Bahama, thinks the government could develop a basic framework for the attraction, with minimum standards.

"The government should put some registrations in place so the pigs are protected," she continues. "You don't want people riding them or mistreating them. You want to keep it where the animals are well protected."

Hocher, the owner of the Staniel Cay Yacht Club, agrees that the time has definitely come for some controls to ensure the well-being of the pigs, not to mention control of the crowds. For his part, he wants the original pig beach to sustain itself as a kind of national treasure that belongs to the whole community. Staniel Cay has always been a hidden gem. He likes the idea of keeping it special and unique, more tightly controlled, where there are clear regulations in place.

Marc Bekoff, professor emeritus of ecology and evolutionary biology at the University of Colorado and author of more than thirty books, still finds time to teach an animal behavior and emotions course at the Boulder County Jail. He believes animal interaction and broader understanding of this world can help improve our relationships with all living things. *Credit: Caitlin Rockett.*

Is it possible for tour operators, resorts, and other entities in the Bahamas to unite as an association? To create minimum stands and oversight? Not just for Staniel Cay, but for all swimming pigs?

It is certainly a worthy goal to strive for.

All of these changes to the attraction would make a difference, though we could also consider our actual relationship with the pigs.

Marc Bekoff is a professor emeritus of ecology and evolutionary biology at the University of Colorado. As the author of at least thirty books and more than a thousand articles, he lectures internationally on what is going on in the minds of animals, with a particular focus on behavior and how that fits in with humanity.

Let's call him a real-life Doctor Dolittle of the academic world.

In his latest book, *The Animals' Agenda: Freedom, Compassion, and Coexistence in the Human Age*, Bekoff intimately explores what we know about the inner lives of animals. He argues that if we truly want a sustainable relationship, we have to approach the pig from a position of respect. That means more than simply monitoring their food and water; it requires the acknowledgement that they are individual beings with their own agenda.

"I think pigs just want to be free to be pigs," he tells me. "Honestly, I don't think it is all that complex. The animal's agenda is to live in peace and safety in a human-dominated world. To be allowed to be who they are and what they are. We control every aspect of their lives, so that would be their agenda. It is really not much different from our own. I always say, they don't want anything that we don't want. We all want the same thing."

At its core, it's such a simple concept—let pigs be pigs. And yet, for humans it can be so difficult not to interfere, impose our will, and be destructive. As a species, we have come to expect complete dominance over other beings on this planet.

Can we really expect society to treat animals as equals?

Bekoff acknowledges that we aren't all becoming vegetarians, vegans, and human rights activists overnight. There may always be people out there who eat meat, hunt animals, and believe in what many call the "natural order of things."

But if we could change one thing, if we could make one shift in our daily thoughts and interactions with animals, what would it be?

"Accept animals for who they are," he says.

What does that mean? It means don't assume an animal is friendly and wants to be touched, picked up, or cornered. Maybe it's having a bad day. Perhaps it had a fight with another animal or human that day. It could be sick, hungry, or injured. Or more simply, it just doesn't want to be engaged. If humans are ever going to develop a genuine respect for the animal kingdom, there has to be a baseline of understanding that they have feelings, too. As humans, we constantly underestimate the emotions of animals in our interaction with them, according to Bekoff. We assume that because we feel something, or want something, they want it, too.

Or perhaps many of us just don't care enough to try.

It raises the question: is this even possible? Is society capable of this level of sensitivity? We can barely treat fellow humans with respect, let alone a pig.

"I do believe it is possible," Bekoff insists. "It's definitely possible. It just means we are going to have to be more tolerant of who other animals are. We have to learn from them. And we will have to bend to accommodate them in our lives. On one hand, given who we are and how many humans there are, and the different situations we encounter animals in, I know it'll be difficult. But the bottom line is—we can do much better than what we are doing now."

I think most people can agree with that; whether it be modern-day industrial farming or our day-to-day interaction with animals, you don't have to look far to see that humans are capable of horrifying acts. As a society, there are clearly glaring contradictions in our thoughts and treatment of animals.

Our cognitive dissonance is real.

At the same time, there are also plenty of examples of humans, from all walks of life, making a genuine connection with animals. It happens every day with the swimming pigs. It shows that you can appreciate and respect the animal but eat bacon, too.

Many of us are just like Fern from *Charlotte's Web*.

And maybe that is the crux of this issue: we spend too much time pigeonholing people. You are a vegan or vegetarian: you love animals. You eat meat: you don't respect animals. Perhaps, for us to really move forward, we need a more inclusive way of thinking about this issue. It's okay to be like Fern.

Perhaps there is more to animal coexistence than meets the eye.

In addition to Bekoff's teaching, research, hundreds of articles, dozens of books, and international lecture circuit, he teaches an animal behavior and emotions course at the Boulder County Jail in Colorado as part of the institution's educational and life skills programming. I'm told it is the only class like it in the whole world, apart from a similar program in Italy, apparently modeled after Bekoff's sessions.

He has done it for more than sixteen years.

It's not the most glamorous gig, teaching animal behavior once a week to convicted felons, some of whom have inflicted unspeakable harm on people.

The sessions are light and informal. They might watch a movie by *National Geographic*, or they will have a discussion about animals, or perhaps they will all write or draw. Bekoff uses examples of animal behavior, such as working collectively and conflict resolution, to help them think about the world differently and make changes in their own lives. Something about the innocence and purity of animals makes them an effective mirror for the human soul. Bekoff calls it "bridging the empathy gap," or teaching people to expand their capacity of compassion.

"Learning about animal behavior, these guys tell me it has softened them," he says. "It is developing a sensitivity and sensibility that can be expanded to humans."

Could the swimming pigs serve a similar purpose?

Bekoff certainly believes so. He argues that Pig Beach is a test tube for experimenting with interaction between human and animal. Of thinking about animals in a different way—overcoming stereotypes, promoting compassion.

And not just any animal—the pig—in all of its rich cultural, sociological, and religious significance. Maybe, just maybe, a secluded, blissful island in Exuma, populated only by pigs, can be an example to us all: a catalyst for change.

Not just a change in how we treat pigs, but how we treat one another.

Acknowledgments

There are many people I want to thank who helped make this book possible. First, I want to thank my wife, the mother of our twin girls, for her support and patience.

I also want to mention Peter Nicholson, who, among other things, has always been a loyal friend and supporter. Diane Phillips, for her friendship, thoughtful advice, and foreword contribution. Thanks to Howie Sonnenschein, the "Instagram team," and many others for sharing their photos with me.

There were also many enthusiastic contributors to this book, and without their support, it would not have been possible: Ventoi Bethune, Joanne Lefson (and Pigcasso), Olivia Mikhail, Rachel & Jillian Crockett, Dr. Jordan Rosenblum, Harbour Safaris, Dr. Walid Saleh, Amanda Parlee, Carolina Fernandez, the Make-A-Wish Foundation, Dr. Marc Bekoff, Dr. Hal Herzog, Tyrone Munroe, Cordell Thompson, Captain Jerry Lewless, Judy Hurlock, Jeffrey Yoskowitz, Elvis Rolle, and the Bahamas Humane Society. I am equally indebted to the wonderful people of Staniel Cay, such as David Hocher, Vivian Rolle, Bernadette Chamberlain, Veronica Rolle, Wayde Nixon, Don Rolle, Kuenson Rolle, Adam Stewart, Bruce Pinder, Nigel Bowe, Ryan Schiedel, Anthony Reckley, and many others, for sharing their stories.

I was also greatly assisted by Charlie Smith and Kevin Taylor, who helped film our movies on the swimming pigs.

Thank you to my agents at Acacia House—Bill Hanna and Kathy Olenski—for their hard work and wise council.

Never in my life did I think I would write a book about swimming pigs. What began as an amusing story turned into an eye-opening consideration of our relationship with the pig and the wider animal kingdom. It taught me that sometimes the simplest ideas can also be the most complex.